Quality in Canadian Public Education

A Critical Assessment

Quality in Canadian Public Education

A Critical Assessment

Contributing Editors
Hugh A. Stevenson
The University of Western Ontario
J. Donald Wilson
The University of British Columbia

The Falmer Press
(A member of the Taylor & Francis Group)
London ● New York ● Philadelphia

UK   The Falmer Press, Falmer House, Barcombe, Lewes, East Sussex,
          BN8 5DL

USA   The Falmer Press, Taylor & Francis Inc., 242 Cherry Street,
          Philadelphia, PA 19106–1906

First published 1988

Library of Congress Cataloging-in-Publication Data

Quality in Canadian public education : a critical assessment /
    contributing editors, Hugh A. Stevenson, J. Donald Wilson.
        p. cm.
    Bibliography: p.
    Includes index.
    ISBN 1–85000–325–4 : $40.00.   ISBN 1–85000–326–2 (pbk.) :
$24.00
        1. Education—Canada—Aims and objectives—Congresses.   2.
Public schools—Canada—Congresses.   3. Teachers—Training of—
Canada—Congresses.   4. Universities and colleges—Canada—
Curricula—Congresses.   I. Stevenson, Hugh A., 1935–   . II. Wilson,
J. Donald.
LA412.Q344 1988
371'.01'0971—dc 19   87–33066
                                                                        CIP

Jacket design by Caroline Archer

Typeset in 10½/13 Caledonia by
Imago Publishing Ltd, Thame, Oxon

*Printed and bound in Great Britain by
Redwood Burn Limited, Trowbridge, Wiltshire.*

Contents

Contents

Contributors

DANIEL R. BIRCH is Vice-President (Academic), a Professor and former Dean of the Faculty of Education at The University of British Columbia. He has also been Dean of the Faculty of Education and Associate Vice-President (Academic) at Simon Fraser University.

GEORGE E. CONNELL is President of The University of Toronto. Dr Connell, a biochemist, has taught and conducted research at The University of Toronto, and has served as President of The University of Western Ontario.

HARRY K. FISHER is Director General of The Council of Ministers of Education, Canada and a former Deputy Minister of Education and of Colleges and Universities in Ontario.

VALÉRIEN HARVEY is a Professor of Educational Administration and former Dean of the Faculté d' éducation at the Université de Sherbrooke.

NORMAN HENCHEY is a Professor in the Department of Administration and Policy Studies in the Faculty of Education at McGill University.

NAOMI HERSOM is President of Mount Saint Vincent University. She has been a teacher, school administrator, Professor and Dean of Education serving in schools and universities in four provinces in Western Canada.

J.W. GEORGE IVANY is Vice-President (Academic), Professor of Education and former Dean of the Faculty of Education at Simon Fraser University. He is also a former Dean of Education at Memorial University of Newfoundland.

MICHAEL J.B. JACKSON is Chairman of The Graduate School of Education at Bishop's University.

DAVID L. JOHNSTON has been Principal of McGill University since 1979. Dr Johnston is a former Professor and Dean of the Faculty of Law at The University of Western Ontario. Currently he is serving as President of The Association of Universities and Colleges of Canada and of the Conférence des Recteurs et des Principaux des Universités du Québec.

Contributors

K. GEORGE PEDERSEN is President of The University of Western Ontario. Dr Pedersen has been Dean of Education and Vice-President (Academic) at The University of Victoria and President of both Simon Fraser University and The University of British Columbia.

DAVID F. ROBITAILLE is a Professor of Mathematics Education and Head of the Department of Mathematics and Science Education in the Faculty of Education at The University of British Columbia.

DORIS W. RYAN is a Professor in the field of educational administration and Assistant Director (Field Services and Research) at The Ontario Institute for Studies in Education.

BERNARD J. SHAPIRO is Deputy Minister of Education for the Province of Ontario. He has been a Dean of the Faculty of Education and Vice-President (Academic) at The University of Western Ontario and Director of The Ontario Institute for Studies in Education.

NANCY M. SHEEHAN is Dean of Education at The University of British Columbia and a Professor in the Department of Social and Educational Studies. She came to UBC from The University of Calgary in 1987 where she held a number of academic and administrative appointments.

A. E. SOLES retired in 1985 as Deputy Minister of Universities, Science and Communications for the Province of British Columbia. Throughout his career in education and the public service he played a major role in developing the B.C. system of community colleges. He died while this book was in production.

HUGH A. STEVENSON is a Professor in the Educational Policy Studies Division of the Faculty of Education at The University of Western Ontario.

J. DONALD WILSON is a Professor in the Department of Social and Educational Studies in the Faculty of Education at The University of British Columbia.

Foreword

Each year The Association of Universities and Colleges of Canada (AUCC) holds two meetings for the Executive Heads of the 85 degree-granting institutions that are members. On these occasions the Presidents and Principals usually devote one and a half days to consideration of some relevant aspect of higher education in addition to conducting the business of the Association. Early in his two-year term as President of AUCC, David L. Johnston, Principal of McGill University, put forward the notion that members of the Association should consider critically the quality of Canadian public education and ways in which institutions of higher education might make positive contributions to the enterprise. The Board of AUCC approved his idea and K. George Pedersen, President of The University of Western Ontario, was asked to take the necessary initiatives to organize a meeting that addressed the issues.

The conference took place in Hamilton, Ontario on March 4 and 5, 1987 and this book records for consideration by a broader audience the papers that were presented and the remarks of respondents. As well, the editors have included a paper by A.E. Soles, prepared originally in his capacity as a consultant to the Faculty of Education at Western, because it addresses aspects of education related to public schools, teachers, students and administrators that were not discussed fully at the Hamilton conference.

From the outset, the organizers realized that a comprehensive assessment of Canadian public education could not be accomplished in the limited time available at the conference. With this fact in mind, the program was organized to introduce members of the AUCC to major aspects of the historical and contemporary background in the opening session and to conclude in the final session with an examination of public education's future prospects. As well, several intervening, complementary themes linking directly elementary, secondary and post-secondary sectors were arranged to highlight aspects of education where Canadian universities have well-known responsibilities. This book is essentially organized along similar lines and readers should consider it as an initial and necessarily incomplete examination of the complex interrelated themes that shape the quality of Canadian public education today.

We hope that the collection will give other educators from all sectors, members of all levels of government and representatives of public and private interest groups, the opportunity to consider with us the many serious concerns that emerged in Hamilton as well as other issues that were merely identified as requiring further critical investigation. In this spirit, members of the AUCC concluded their Hamilton meeting by resolving to develop a policy statement on the nature and quality of public education and how universities might play a proper role in relation to these issues. This statement should be made public about the same time that *Quality in Canadian Public Education: A Critical Assessment* is published. The most positive result would be if others recognize the challenges discussed in Hamilton and take action to make changes towards improving the quality of education at all levels.

Many of the conference papers are far from optimistic that Canada is prepared sufficiently well to meet the identifiable educational and related political, social, economic and cultural challenges that exist now and others that lie ahead for the nation. Where hope is held out, it is offered both speculatively and very cautiously. Optimism, where it appears in the papers, the commentaries and the references, is guarded with qualifications pointing to the need for fundamental changes of one kind or another.

As editors we have made no attempt to alter the points of view expressed by contributors or their style which is often somewhat informal and conversational given the nature of their presentations at the conference. It has been impossible, however, to avoid asking ourselves, 'Does a crisis exist in Canadian education?' Recently, other nations facing similar problems with similar provisions in place for public education have answered with a resounding 'yes', and have begun to make essential reforms. The question was certainly on our minds during the Hamilton conference and no doubt it occurred to others who were present. With allowances made for the different ways that nations identify, assess and address public education difficulties, our conclusion is also 'yes' but with specifically Canadian qualifications.

Our federated nation makes resolution of education problems necessarily fragmented. Even so, some issues such as our research capacity, our educative reactions to the computer-communications revolution, and our place in the race for international intellectual and economic competitiveness have been widely recognized and they are beginning to receive widespread attention. Currently reduced levels of funding in several sectors are seen by many to constitute a serious crisis. Other critical issues such as questions of governance, cultural problems, complex social concerns, and those of professional education and organization are raised in the articles and the references that authors have consulted. Since many of these concerns are not well-known or widely understood our selective bibliography is deliberately extensive. Overall, in our judgement, the papers present a timely warning to Canadians that many improvements are needed in education if the nation is to share with other countries in the most positive aspects of this rapidly changing world. At best, we have a narrow window of opportunity remaining open to us.

As editors we must point out that our views and those of other contributors to this collection should not be attributed to members of The Association of Universities and Colleges of Canada. In due course, their position will be made known in the policy statement that is in the course of preparation as this book goes to press.

Also, we wish to thank the authors and other contributors at the AUCC conference for their cooperation and assistance. In particular, we thank Rosemary Cavan, Director of Communications at AUCC, for her part in organizing the conference and Diane MacDonald of the Office of Institutional Planning and Budgeting at The University of Western Ontario who, in her own time, helped us to prepare the manuscript for publication. Finally, we are indebted to the editorial and production staff of Falmer Press; we wish particularly to thank Malcolm Clarkson, Managing Director and Ivor Goodson, Executive Director at Falme, for their encouragement and assistance.

Hugh A. Stevenson
J. Donald Wilson
October 1987

Introduction

K. George Pedersen

The Association of Universities and Colleges of Canada is hardly an organization where it is necessary to attempt to articulate the importance of providing high quality educational services. In historical terms, public mass education is very recent on the scene and Canada, along with our neighbour to the south, has made an important contribution to this impressive and noble social experiment. Canadians have typically given high priority to the development of a strong educational system, recognizing that such an investment in human capital has important social, economic and cultural consequences for all of us. In this context, many of us recall with great affection the halcyon days of the 1960s when support for education was at an all-time high.

Recent shifts in the world economy, with its high level of dependence on the scientific and technological activities associated with the evolving communications and high-tech revolution, may well herald a revival of interest in education comparable to that of the 1960s. A general recognition throughout the Western developed world that future economic success will be very much dependent on highly skilled manpower is cause for some optimism for those of us involved in education, at least relative to the situation which has existed for the past decade or more.

It is of importance, when considering the educational system, to think in terms of how such services should be provided and who benefits from them. Each of us is aware that there are direct educational benefits which fall to an individual and that such benefits are, at least in part, related to the level of educational attainment. In fact, there is an almost perfect positive relationship between level of schooling and income earned. Furthermore, occupation and social status are very closely interrelated with education.

But, of course, it is not just the individual who benefits from an educated body politic. Society itself must take steps to ensure that it has adequate supplies of skilled and informed manpower. Indeed, it is precisely because of this need for informed citizens that we have a public school system at all. Were we interested only in the individual or personal benefits that befall people with a sound education, it is very likely that in a country like Canada we would leave the educational system to the private sector. In order for any form of organized society to progress, it must have the means whereby educated individuals can be prepared in order to allow them to participate fully as citizens. The fact that there are two important beneficiaries of education (the individual and the society) ensures that it will always be difficult to make decisions about new directions for public education.

The provision of educational services in Canada is also made more difficult because of the particular form of federal government that we have created. Assigning the provision of educational services to the provinces has very effectively removed an important lever of public policy from the federal government. Just the multiplicity of euphemisms employed at the federal level in relation to programs that are essentially educational in nature is explicit testimony of its own. Clarity of function and articulation within the educational community are not attributes for which the Canadian system of education is known.

The preparation of teachers for our Canadian public schools is an issue which has been long-standing in its resolution. Moving such professional preparation onto university campuses has been handled in different ways in each of the provinces. Where teacher training should be offered, whether the actual function is a craft or a profession, and who within each university campus carries the overall responsibility for teacher education are but some of the unresolved aspects of the profession. The recency of arrival of teacher education on many university campuses, the limited understanding of the actual teaching–learning process, and the overall lower status of schools of education within the university setting suggest that the preparation of teachers is something less than first-order priority within our university system. If the latter assertion is accurate, and I firmly believe that it is, one cannot help but be both surprised and concerned. Surely the university, if for no other reason than self-interest in the products being produced by our elementary and secondary schools, has a great deal at stake with respect to teacher preparation. Yet it is the rare institution of higher learning that places a high priority on its teacher education program, taking, for example, the point of view that such preparation is an important institution-wide responsibility. It is probably also worth noting that the large majority of the responsibility for teacher preparation which is assumed by the university is restricted to pre-service work, with only limited recognition of the importance of professional development in the field of elementary and secondary school teaching.

Research in an applied field like education is in the infancy of its development. This is to be expected, given that the conceptual base, building as it does on the behavioral and social sciences, is not well established. Added to that observation is the unfortunate situation in Canada whereby very few basic social scientists choose to focus their research interests on the field of education. That we have no James S. Colemans or Theodore W. Schultzs is surprising, given that public education typically ranks number two on the expenditure side of each province. Without such scientific support from the broader university community, it is a matter of open debate as to whether the levels of scholarship will be attained. Closely allied is the imperative of ensuring that graduate work in the field of education is dependent in large measure for its theoretical underpinnings on the basic social sciences.

To conclude, if we are convinced that Canada's future success is heavily dependent on our capacity to deliver educational services, then our universities have greater responsibilities than are currently being assumed. Literacy, basic and otherwise, quantitative and verbal, will be the stock in trade in this newly arrived communications revolution. I urge each of you, in the two days ahead, to think through carefully the role that should be assumed by AUCC and its member institutions in our efforts to improve the overall quality of public education.

1 'Indoor Toilets in 744 Schools': Themes of Progress in Canadian Educational History*

J. Donald Wilson

The public school is one of the central institutions of the modern State. Since its creation in Canada almost 150 years ago, it has increasingly displaced the centrality of the family and the church in the education of children. While these educative agents still have a role to play in most children's lives, there is no denying that for most people the school has become synonymous with education. Consequently the school's role in Western society today may be considered to be similar in its centrality to the church in the Middle Ages. Moreover, as the 1936–37 Programme of Studies for the Elementary Schools of British Columbia so succinctly put it: 'From the point of view of society, the schools in any state exist to develop citizens, or subjects, according to the prevailing or dominating ideals of the state or society . . .'[1] By the turn of the century the school and church had as their central role in Canadian life the provision of intellectual and moral guidance for the nation. 'The central institutions for social improvement thus became,' as Doug Owram has recently stated, 'not the state, which could at best minister only to external matters, but the classroom and the pulpit.'[2] It is in this light that we should view the educational reform of the turn of the century, the New Education era, and in particular the stress on civics and citizenship education in the 1920s.

Originally schools were products of single communities, set up by parents in accordance with their wishes for their children's education. Teachers were hired usually by three trustees elected to office by the parents and other ratepayers in the community. But from the 1840s in British North America that all changed and schools became components of educational systems governed from the provincial capital. State-supported mass education would guarantee universal literacy which it was held would promote popular enlightenment and rational behaviour on the part of the masses. In addition education was to engender a 'proper appreciation (and acceptance) of one's place in society and to promote shared values and

5

customs, thereby ensuring social stability.'[3] But the aims of school author-ities and politicians was one thing and the motivation parents had for sending their children to school was often quite another. The official agenda always had a set of outcomes in mind designed to serve society's needs. But parental goals and the 'subjective experience of the educand,' as Brian Simon says, often produced unintended consequences.[4] For example, that most native Indian leaders in Canada today are products of Indian residential schools is an ironic commentary on the social control hypothesis of educational history.

When it comes to a discussion of the history of education in Canada (the theme of this paper) it is important to be cognizant that there is no one history, as C.E. Phillips implied in his monumental *The Development of Public Education in Canada*, but rather many histories.[5] To illustrate what I mean, one feminist scholar has argued that the history of Canadian education is at the very least two histories — one history for males and a different one for females.[6] Aside from the obvious topics of sex-segregated schooling and male-dominated post-secondary education for over a century, one can point to the feminization of elementary teaching in the face of the evolution of patriarchal rule by principals, inspectors, superintendents, and Department of Education bureaucrats. Patriarchal rule is of course equally evident in the history of Canadian higher education and remains true today. If we take another topic, the history of elementary and secondary education in Canada, we find that the story holds entirely different implications for the children of non-British/non-French ancestry than for the children of the dominant majority. For the former, school was (and still is) an agent of assimilation for immigrant children. For other Canadian children their schooling was entirely segregated from the mainstream public schools, as in the case of native Indians and Blacks. In British Columbia efforts, which proved unsuccessful, were made to segregate Chinese and Japanese children and/or limit the amount of schooling they could get. Other religio-ethnic groups, such as Mennonites, Hutterites and Doukhobors, sought to be left alone with varying degrees of success. Evangelical Christians and in some provinces Roman Catholics have removed their children from the public schools altogether. Thus, once again, there are two major histories here.

How can one talk sensibly in thirty minutes about 'Canada's historical record in public education'? Clearly the topic as given is too vast. I have decided instead to choose one theme of many that run through the history of education in this country, namely the theme of progress, and to confine my examples to English-Canadian education. I am convinced, however, that much the same case could be made for Quebec in the same time period.

The following is an exchange between Premier Joey Smallwood and an interviewer in respect to certain accomplishments under his premiership. The interview occurred in the late sixties.

Question	84?
Smallwood	Eighty-four.
	In all Newfoundland and Labrador.
	84.
Question	84 what?
Smallwood	84 schools with indoor toilets.

That was Newfoundland on the day that I became Premier. Today: 838 schools have indoor toilets. We have not in those years produced any new or original educational theory, philosophy or practices. But we have put indoor toilets in 744 [*sic*] schools that didn't have them. That's progress.

The above is as fitting a text as any for my talk today. Basically it singles out two important themes in Canadian educational history — one major and the other minor. The major one is, of course, the notion of progress in Canadian educational development. Smallwood's response points to the various interpretations that can be and have been put on progress in education. He obviously felt satisfied to measure progress in terms of material things, such as number and size of schools, textbooks, school buses, ventilation and indoor plumbing. But, interestingly, his answer also referred to the other kind of progress in Canadian education, namely the evolution of new educational theory or improved practices in implementing the educational process. With respect to post-Confederation Newfoundland, Smallwood contrasted the progress in material things related to schooling with the failure to produce 'any new or original educational theory, philosophy or practice.' For him the absence of the latter was no great loss for Newfoundland. But, frankly speaking, Smallwood's assessment on this score might quite validly be applied to the rest of Canada for the period of the last 150 years over which time our present system of public education has evolved. Authorities as prestigious as the authors of the OECD Report on Canadian education in 1976 came to essentially the same conclusion; 'reforms in [Canadian] education are almost totally pragmatic, or so generally conceived and relying so heavily on United States, British, and French models, more or less adapted to Canadian conditions, that the opportunity for conflict is, for all practical purposes, excluded.' This conclusion in turn led the OECD commissioners to assert that 'Canadian educational policy may be one of the least "politicized" in the world.'[8] The above observation also helps to explain the basically conservative nature of Canadian education, a factor summed up by one foreign observer as the 'prosaic sanity' of both Canadian society and education.[9]

Of course, there is yet another way to view progress and that may also be applicable to Canadian education. The view holds that we get an impression of change, of things being 'new' and progressing when in actual fact it is simply an illusion but one which is calculated to give us the impression of progress and change. The American social scientist Russell Jacoby has summed up this situation well in the following words:

> The evident acceleration of production and consumption in the economic sphere, and hysteria and frenzy in life itself, does not preclude the possibility that a fixed society is simply spinning faster. If this is true, the application of planned obsolescence to thought itself has the same merit as its application to consumer goods; the new is not only shoddier than the old, it fuels an obsolete social system that staves off its replacement by manufacturing the illusion that it is perpetually new.[10]

Let us leave aside for the time being any discussion of the notion of the illusion of change.

Canadians, like Americans, have over the past century been wont to attribute societal progress, both social and economic, to the expanding public school system including more recently the post-secondary system. A Maritime critic in 1842 astutely observed the correlation between popular education and the attainment of economic progress:

> The improvement of the mind adds to the skill and manipulation of the hand, and thus enlarges its powers of production. The science and skill of the mechanic [skilled worker] are a part of his annual income ... and of course of the wealth of the state. If the hand of one man can be formed and trained to do the labour of ten, the food he consumes gives a ten-fold value to the products of its industry. The cultivation of the mind increases skill, multiplies inventions, and gives new power and facility to the mechanic. The intellect of a nation becomes thus its richest mine of Gold .... By making the system general, so as to embrace all, every mind and every talent is more likely to be developed, and the national powers of production to be of course increased.[11]

It is remarkable how closely this line of argument resembles the rationale behind the highly-touted human capital theory as expounded by the Economic Council of Canada in the mid-1960s. This prestigious and highly respected body concluded that once a high level of physical capital accumulation and advanced industrial organization had been achieved, further economic growth depended mainly on technical innovation; and, in turn, technical innovation was seen as a product of highly skilled and qualified 'brain-power'. Hence, more educated people with higher levels of formal education meant more productivity, and more productivity meant higher standards of living, something all good Canadians presumably aspired to. One need not dwell on the fact with this audience that vast sums of public money were poured into all levels of Canadian public education in the mid to late sixties precisely because of the confident assurances of success voiced by the Economic Council of Canada. In the period between 1960 and 1975 expenditures on all levels of public education including universities increased sevenfold. By 1969 Canada led the major industrial countries in the share of its Gross National Product devoted to public expenditures on education. Its figure of 7.6 per cent compared favourably with the Soviet Union at 7.3 per cent, bettered the United States at 6.3 per cent, and almost doubled the percentage figure for France, Japan, and West Germany respectively.[12]

To illustrate that this theme of schooling and economic progress was a continuous one in Canadian education from the mid-nineteenth century, consider the following 1926 tribute paid to the school by the Dominion Bureau of Statistics.

> On the whole, therefore, the progress made since 1911 and especially the very marked progress since 1891, may be said to have been brought about solely by the schools of Canada, and that in spite of increasing difficulties, the advantages of improved settlement being more than counterbalanced by the disadvantages of the immigration of illiterate persons. The active instruments of progress in educational status may, therefore... be reduced to one — the school...[13]

Such a statement would have warmed the hearts of the long deceased school promoters of the mid-nineteenth century. The central role of the school in the economic and social development of the country was the point of all their educational reforms.

In point of fact, the faith in public education's benefits seems in no way to have abated over the past decade. British Columbia's newly appointed Minister of Advanced Education and job training is optimistic about the prospects for higher education. 'From what I have seen,' he concluded in January, 1987, 'the students are getting an excellent education and the faculty and professors are doing a good job. The public seems generally happy with the universities, colleges, and training institutions.' For the minister, that 'advanced education' has been lumped together with 'job training' in his new ministry is no anomaly. 'I think it's a natural step,' Hagen retorted, 'because the two go hand in hand. There's a real interaction between the two.'[14] This is a generally accepted view today among politicians.

If we accept Premier Smallwood's contention that Canada has produced no new or original educational theory, philosophy or practice, then we can define and discuss progress in Canadian education in terms of technological, pedagogical and institutional elements. Examples of technological innovations having impact on public education are blackboards, indoor toilets, films and computers; of pedagogical innovations are uniform texts, graded classrooms, child-centred education, team teaching and open-area classrooms; of institutional innovations are multi-grade/multi-roomed schools, rural school consolidation, technical and commercial schools, composite high schools, and community colleges. All three types of innovation were often linked in any particular reform period. To take but one example: the spread of blackboard use in Upper Canada. This technological innovation accompanied by the introduction of uniform textbooks allowed for the shift of emphasis from individual, rote recitations from the pupil's own book to the simultaneous method of teaching. The importance of this new method has been well described by a recent scholar of this innovation.

> Simultaneous teaching was ... supposed to be more stimulating to children and, according to the reformed pedagogy, teachers were not only to instruct and control their pupils but to interest them... Whole classes were now expected to rivet their attention on the teacher, or on the increasingly ubiquitous blackboards, and to work together.[15]

The entire ecology of the classroom was fundamentally altered by the apparently simple innovation of a modest blackboard accommodated on an easel. (By World War I school suppliers advocated school room walls almost entirely covered with boards).[16] Rote learning and the recitation method came to be replaced by a collective response and a new focus on the teacher. Attention came to be centred on the written rather than the spoken word and the blackboard necessitated greater silence and classroom control. All told, classroom relations were fundmentally altered among students and between students and teacher. The effectiveness of the education department's pressure favouring blackboards is well illustrated in the work of Alison Prentice showing the adoption of blackboards by Upper Canadian schools in the decade from 1856 to 1866. The spread in the use of this technological/pedagogical innovation in the span of one decade is quite remarkable.[17] One is reminded of the almost reverse effects of a highly recommended American-inspired innovation of the late sixties, namely the open-area classroom. In this innovation blackboard use was discouraged since, among other reasons,wall-space was at a premium. Instead of teacher-centred instruction, groupwork was stressed. Peer cooperation replaced individual student competitiveness; student-centred learning in groups meant by definition an absence of silence and little 'simultaneous' teaching for the whole class. And finally, the open-area concept led to a breaking down of age/grade classification as older children were encouraged to assist younger ones.

The theme of progress in Canadian educational history tends to imply that change and reform have been of a 'progressive' nature. There is something reassuring about the word 'progressive' as opposed to its most often applied counterpart, 'traditional'. Perhaps that is why some political parties like to use such a term in their names. However, despite talk by both contemporaries and historians about the progressive nature of Canadian education, the fact is that it has remained essentially conservative. The most representative figures in Canadian educational history are not Charles Duncombe, Hubert Newland, Marshall McLuhan and Lloyd Dennis, but rather Egerton Ryerson, Peter Sandiford, George Weir and Hilda Neatby. While the latter group favoured change, the reforms they advocated were intended to preserve the 'prosaic sanity' of Canadian society or as Vincent Massey once put it, to preserve 'the elements of human stability' which he contended were most 'highly developed' in the British Isles and north-western Europe.[18] The Ontario school inspector in commenting on the progressive curriculum revisions of 1937 had much the same in mind when he commented that the aim of the revision was 'to interest the child in his work, so that he wants to do what we want him to do.'[19] That sentiment would certainly have appealed to both Vincent Massey and Hilda Neatby not to mention many critics of Canadian schools today. The report of the Massey Commission in 1951 and Neatby's best-seller *So Little For the Mind* in 1953 carried the same messsage. Canada was in grave danger of being Americanized and democratized and the greatest culprit was the sort of permissive, anti-intellectual, anti-cultural and amoral education advocated by the supporters of the American pragmatist John Dewey. If Canada was to be saved from the excesses of American life, the influence of American progressivism must be stemmed, and the British sense of order, stability and hierarchy restored.

That Massey and Neatby were critical of the materialism and anti-intellectualism of Canadian society in the 1950s and the educational system that fed into it had its counterpart at the turn of the century in George M. Grant. Speaking in 1901, Grant lamented, 'Judging by the tone of the public press, I for one am often saddened beyond the power of words to express . . . .' The problem was a 'vulgar and insolent materialism of thought and life.'[20] Grant's concerns seemed well founded if we can judge from the principles underlying the 'social efficiency' movement of the time. In 1915 an official Ontario teachers' manual expressed four purposes for this sort of education: an appreciation of liberty and the need to vote intelligently; the dissemination of knowledge for 'social progress and happiness;' the enhancement of the welfare of society which was much more important than enhancing 'the individual advantage of pupils;' and industrial efficiency to be promoted by means of practical subjects which would 'make each individual a productive social unit.'[21] A similar sentiment, indicative of the nation-wide acceptance of social efficiency, was a statement in 1930 by Langley, B.C., high school principal, H. L. Mazer:

> A young life properly 'fitted into' the niche of industry to which it naturally belongs wears soon into an integral and smoothly functioning cog of industrial and social progress. It requires no adjusting, no oiling, no refining. Improperly 'fitted into,' as is often

the case ... this young life becomes a slashing gear, a loose bolt, that soon must drop into the discard of unemployment. Or worse still, it threatens and impedes industrial and social progress, and thereby the peace of mind and well-being of the whole national life.[22]

The same current of conservative nostalgia was not far beneath the surface of the back-to-the-basics movement of a decade ago. The euphoria of the mid-sixties gave way to the disenchantment about public education in the mid-seventies. In the sixties there was a widespread sentiment holding that education was an intrinsic good; everyone could benefit from having a good education. Similarly, at the societal level, public education was seen by many as the main instrument for bringing about a better society. Curious, inquisitive students prepared to challenge old-fashioned views would result, it was held, in a more innovative and egalitarian society. Thus all political parties favoured equality of access to post-secondary education so as to improve access for women, those from lower income groups, immigrants and native people. By the mid-seventies, the above contentions were being seriously questioned by a restless public. Great sums of money had been spent, but the promised results in socio-economic advance had not been attained. Instead of stressing the liberating, individual advantages of schooling, the school was looked to in a more traditional, instrumental way as a panacea to solve immediate problems. Unemployment rates were high; so schooling should be linked more closely to work. Rates of crime and public immorality were on the increase, so the school should return to its nineteenth century role as an expediter of moral reform. The school should take the lead in combatting 'thorny' social problems, such as drug-taking and sexual permissiveness.

The parallels between mid-nineteenth century views of social reform and the last decade are quite startling. In that era, the poor, ignorant, unemployed and criminal were lumped together as a degraded class. What we speak of today as the 'deprived' (in economic terms), they spoke of then as the 'depraved' (in moral terms). Back then, cities were thought to be threatened by a criminal class — the 'dangerous classes' — when in fact no such class existed. The likelihood of this class propagating a whole new class of criminals was held to be a very present danger. The social disease as represented by this class could best be cured, according to the authorities who mattered, by reliance on education if not always for the depraved then most certainly for their children. Fundamental political and economic change was proposed by some, such as the Chartists in England, but discounted or opposed by most. Universal schooling was the preferred solution. In the 1980s not much has changed. Issues of crime, poverty and unemployment (all of which seem to be increasing) lead to moral condemnation of the poor. Welfare benefits, it is held by some politicians, should only go to those who 'want to work'. Even the solutions proposed are reminiscent of the mid-nineteenth century: reimpose capital punishment (a 'free vote' was to be held in Parliament this year); punish criminals not the victims of crimes; and introduce school reforms: crack down on teachers, replace permissiveness and choice with discipline and compulsory courses, introduce consumer, drug and sex education, reintroduce some form of moral education with a view to character-building among students, gear schooling and even university education to job training so as to offset high unemployment. All this makes one wonder how much we have learned from the past about what exactly the school can be expected to accomplish. Clearly, despite all our good intentions, the school cannot reasonably be expected to act as a panacea for society's social and economic ills. It should be obvious, for example, that schools do not create jobs.

This might be a good point to return to Russell Jacoby's quote about the illusion of change and progress, the sense people have that something new is unfolding when in actuality 'a fixed society,' as Jacoby asserts, 'is simply spinning faster.' Recent studies by Neil Sutherland, Robert Patterson and George Tomkins suggest, for example, that the much-touted progressive education of the inter-war years never in fact got implemented in the classroom.[23] Many curriculum changes and programme revisions were announced in the 1930s right across Canada, but when you actually check out the classroom of the time you find that very little had changed from the previous decade or even from the pre-World War I era for that matter. The formal discipline theory of studies which Putman and Weir condemned in British Columbia in their 1925 report continued to predominate in Canadian schools of the late thirties and forties. Learning out of a book, similarly condemned as old-fashioned, persisted despite fanfare about the project method or the enterprise.[24] Drills on the formal parts of grammar and arithmetic or the facts of history and geography remained, we are told, central to the pedagogy of those subjects, even though group-learning in a cooperative ambiance had been advocated by the New Education proponents. *So Little For the Mind*, Hilda Neatby's diatribe against what she called the pervasiveness of progressive education in Canadian schools by the 1950s, wasn't wrong provided you accept she was addressing the intentions of Canadian educators as reflected in their programmes of study and policy statements. However, if you are to consider what actually got implemented, what got into the classroom, Neatby's book is profoundly wrong. Both Sutherland and Tomkins tell us that 'formalism', by which they mean those elements most hated by progressives such as book-learning, drills and memorization, persisted throughout the second quarter of the twentieth century.

Sutherland's study of elementary schooling in the inter-war period includes the following descriptions:

> Even those who enjoyed it [school] then, now recall a system
> that put its rigor into rote learning, the times tables, the spelling

words, the "Lady of the Lake," the capes and bays, "the twelve adverbial modifiers (of place, of reason, of time . . .)," and the Kings and Queens. It was a system based on teachers talking and pupils listening, a system that discouraged independent thought, a system that provided no opportunity to be creative, a system that blamed rather than praised, a system that made no direct or purposed effort to build a sense of self-worth . . . .[25]

All of this is far removed from the democracy, anti-intellectualism and amorality which Neatby accused John Dewey of perpetrating on Canadian school children.

Further evidence of the immense gulf between declared intentions as reflected in curriculum guidelines and actual classroom practice can be found in Melinda McCracken's memoir of attending Churchill High School in Winnipeg in the mid-fifties.

The lecture method of teaching, with the teacher standing at the front of the room and the class subserviently listening, didn't help. The teacher had control of the class; to ask a question, the student raised his hand, and hoped the teacher would pick up on it. There was no encouragement or discussion. Kids were forbidden to talk to one another in class. You were supposed to sit there passively and have your little mind moulded.

The teacher took the textbook and went through it in the year. The teacher would set a page of problems for the day, or a chapter to read. You would take them home, do the problems, read the chapter and come back the next day, when the teacher would go over the problems with the class, have members of the class read parts of the chapter, explain it a bit and then set another chapter and more problems. You weren't supposed to read beyond a specified page, or even so much as peek at the next page of problems, and so you didn't. The teacher took the responsibility for getting you through the book. If you did it yourself, you'd spoil it for yourself, because you'd only have to go through it all again at the pace of the whole class. It wasn't much of a challenge. You'd sit there listening to each tick of the minute hand on the big white clock overhead, as it inched towards the end of the period.[26]

Once again McCracken's description of things reiterates the 'triumph of formalism,' as Sutherland calls it, ironically at the very time that Neatby lamented the supposedly widespread use of progressive education in Canadian schools. The boring routine, regimentation and passive learning described above starkly resemble the very circumstances Dewey most deplored about American classrooms a half century earlier. Canadian-style democracy and British traditions were hardly under siege if we can accept McCracken's recollection as typical.

A final note on the sweeping reforms of the sixties is probably in order since our own era is still reacting to the massive changes of two decades ago. The most long-lasting changes were probably structural, namely the conversion of the secondary school from the screening institution it had been into a retaining institution. In all provinces retention rates for grades nine to eleven shot up 50 to 100 per cent between the late fifties and the early seventies.[27] Today most Canadian youths stay on until the end of grade twelve to acquire that basic credential for a good job (or any job), the high school diploma, and for many the basic admission requirement to some post-secondary institution entailing another two to four years of schooling at a minimum. The other major structural change of the late sixties was the democratization of post-secondary education, that is vastly improved accessibility. This necessitated on the one hand the establishment of dozens of new universities and the expansion of the already existent 'old' universities. Student fees remained low relative to actual costs and student loans and bursaries were widely available to qualified students. For non-university students there was the introduction in almost every province of a new system of community colleges, most of which provided both terminal diploma or university transfer programs.[28] By virtue of these developments the formerly elite nature of Canadian post-secondary education so cherished by Hilda Neatby was smashed. Universities mainly for the leadership training of the sons of the economically privileged became a thing of the past. Young women benefitted most, especially in the province of Quebec, but also much higher percentages of students from lower socio-economic groups gained access to higher education. Many of them were children of post-World War II immigrants. Universities and community colleges in fact became a tertiary level fo public education, a development much deplored recently by the outraged authors of *The Great Brain Robbery*.[29]

As long as economic expansion continued, vast sums of provincial and federal money poured into public education. But the oil crisis in 1973 and subsequent recession were to change all this quite dramatically. The sweeping promises that school reformers and adminstrators had made for education in the sixties remained largely unfulfilled. More and better schools and the young in school longer seemed not to be the answer for unemployment, underemployment and rising crime rates among youth. Parents and taxpayers became critical, contending they were not getting their money's worth despite the rising costs of public education. The situation was made worse by a decline in school enrolment figures, largely for demographic reasons. Thus it became necessary for the first time in history actually to close schools for reason of there being no students. Teacher militancy, sometimes leading to strike action, in the mid-seventies annoyed parents and taxpayers alike. Now school closings led to teacher layoffs and increased levels of unemployment among teachers. Criticism mounted about the perceived decline in uniform standards of school achievement and blame was directed at lazy and incompetent teachers, the abolition of province-wide examinations, and vast student-choice provided by cafeteria-style curricula introduced in the late sixties.

By the mid-eighties a new trend was apparent characterized by more provincial control and less local autonomy. There was a nation-wide return to province-wide testing and standardization and increased uniformity among schools in various parts of a province. 'Accountability' became a new watchword with much closer scrutiny of teachers very evident. Only a small minority of parents were switching their children to private schools but at an increased pace.[30]

To the extent that participation rates are high, it would seem that both students and parents retain a strong faith in the value of formal education.[31] In 1982–83, 99–100 per cent of Canadian elementary school-age children were in elementary schools, 85 per cent of secondary school-age children were in secondary schools and 22 per cent of university-age students were attending post-secondary institutions. Fifty-nine per cent of this last group were in universities.[32] Facts of this sort bespeak a commitment to public education (less than 5 per cent of Canadian children attend private schools) that Egerton Ryerson could only have dreamed of. Canadians may not have produced any new and original philosophy of education in over 150 years, but one may be as proud of the material progress in public education as Joey Smallwood was of his 744 indoor toilets. Perhaps we need some progress of the sort Smallwood had little time for, namely some 'new or original educational theory, philosophy or practices.' Our commitment to common schooling, whether this can be said to be a 'philosophy' or not, remains strong. But so does public criticism, even disillusionment, with the schools. In this respect criticism of the schools closely parallels that of society in general.

Today, unlike the mid-nineteenth century and the turn of the century, Canadian society and consequently its schools are lacking in common belief systems. These common beliefs served in the past to make the various components of public education coherent. As Diane Ravitch has commented about American schools, 'a society that is confused and contentious cannot look to its schools to straighten things out, for the schools will reflect the same confusion and contention.'[33] It seems appropriate somehow to leave the last word to the famous (or infamous) Hall-Dennis Report. In trying to resolve the inherent tensions between the social and individual aims of education, the committee concluded, 'How to provide learning experiences aiming at a thousand different destinies and at the same time to educate toward a common heritage and common citizenship is the basic challenge to our society.'[34] To meet that challenge remains as urgent today as twenty years ago.

Notes

*The author wishes to acknowledge with thanks, the helpful suggestions of Jean Barman.

[1]George S. Tomkins, *A Common Countenance: Stability and Change in the Canadian Curriculum* (Toronto: Prentice-Hall, 1986), p. 155.

[2]Doug Owram, *The Government Generation: Canadian Intellectuals and the State, 1900–1945* (Toronto: University of Toronto Press, 1986), p. 8.

[3]Chad Gaffield, 'History of Education,' *The Canadian Encyclopedia*, vol. 1 (Edmonton: Hurtig, 1985), p. 546.

[4]Brian Simon, 'Can Education Change Society?' in J. Donald Wilson (ed.), *An Imperfect Past: Education and Society in Canadian History* (Vancouver: UBC Curriculum Centre, 1984), p. 45.

[5]Charles E. Phillips, *The Development of Education in Canada* (Toronto: W.J. Gage, 1957), p. xi–xii.

[6]Alison Prentice, 'Towards a Feminist History of Women and Education,' in David C. Jones, *et al.*, (eds.), *Approaches to Educational History* (Winnipeg: University of Manitoba, 1981).

[7]Joseph R. Smallwood, *To You With Affection From Joey* (St. John's, 1969), p. 37. It is perhaps of interest to note that as of 1967–68, there were still slightly more than 200 schools in Newfoundland without indoor toilets. See Table E3 'Selected Statistics of Public Schools in Newfoundland and Labrador, 1949–50 to 1968–69,' *Historical Statistics of Newfoundland and Labrador* (St. John's: Economics and Statistics Division, Department of Finance, 1970), vol. I, pt. 1, p. 97.

[8]Organization for Economic Co-operation and Development, *Reviews of National Policies for Education: Canada* (Paris: OECD, 1976), p. 19. [Hereafter OECD Report, Canada].

[9]Fred Clarke in 1935 as quoted in Tomkins, p. 234.

[10]Russell Jacoby, *Social Amnesia* (Boston: Beacon Press, 1975), p. xviii.

[11]George R. Young, *On Colonial Literature, Science and Education. . .* (Halifax, 1842), as quoted in D.A. Lawr and R.D. Gidney (eds.), *Educating Canadians: A Documentary History of Public Education* (Toronto: Van Nostrand Reinhold, 1973), p. 46.

[12]OECD Report, *Canada*, pp. 28–9.

[13]Quoted in Tomkins, p. 111.

[14]*The Ubyssey*, Jan. 13, 1987, p. 1.

[15]Alison Prentice, 'From Household to School House: The Emergence of the Teacher as Servant of the State,' *Material History Bulletin*, no. 20, p. 22.

[16]*Ibid.*, p. 26.

[17]*Ibid.*, p. 23.

[18]Vincent Massey, *On Being Canadian* (Toronto: J.M. Dent, 1948), pp. 29–30.

[19]Quoted in Tomkins, p. 199.

[20]Owram, p. 15.

[21]Quoted in Tomkins, pp. 115–16.

[22]Quoted in Timothy A. Dunn, 'The Rise of Mass Public Schooling in British Columbia, 1900–1919,' in J.D. Wilson and D.C. Jones (eds.), *Schooling and Society in 20th Century British Columbia* (Calgary: Detselig, 1980), p. 23.

[23]Neil Sutherland, 'The Triumph of 'Formalism': Elementary Schooling in Vancouver From the 1920s to the 1960s,' *B.C. Studies*, no. 69/70 (Spring/summer 1986), pp. 175–210; R. S. Patterson, 'The Canadian Response to Progressive Education,' and 'The Implementation of Progressive Education in Canada, 1930–45' in Nick Kach, *et al.* (eds.), *Essays on Canadian Education* (Calgary: Detselig, 1986), chaps. 4, 5; Tomkins, *op. cit.*, Chapters 10 and 12. For a less negative assessment, see Robert

M. Stamp, 'Canadian High Schools in the 1920s and 1930s: The Social Challenge to the Academic Tradition,' *Historical Papers, 1978* (CHA), pp. 76–94.

[24]Putman, J.H. and G. M. Weir, *Survey of the School System* (Victoria: King's Printer, 1925), pp. 118–21.

[25]Sutherland, pp. 182–83.

[26]Melinda McCracken, *Memories Are Made of This* (Toronto: James Lorimer, 1975), p. 78.

[27]David Munroe, *The Organization and Administration of Education in Canada* (Ottawa: Information Canada, 1974), p. 215.

[28]See John D. Dennison and Paul Gallagher, *Canada's Community Colleges: A Critical Analysis* (Vancouver: UBC Press, 1986).

[29]David J. Bercuson, Robert Bothwell, and J.L. Granatstein, *The Great Brain Robbery* (Toronto: McClelland and Stewart, 1984).

[30]J. Donald Wilson, 'Religion and Education: The Other Side of Pluralism,' in Wilson (ed.), *Canadian Education in the 1980's* (Calgary: Detselig, 1981), Chapter 6; and 'Public Support of Private and Independent Schools in Canada, *Koulu ja Menneisyys* [1986 Yearbook of the Finnish History of Education Society] (Helsinki, 1986), pp. 8–22.

[31]This seems to be true for the United States as well. See David Tyack and Elisabeth Hansot, *Managers of Virtue: Public School Leadership in America, 1820–1980* (New York: Basic Books, 1982), Part III.

[32]'School Systems,' in *The Canadian Encyclopedia*, vol. III, p. 1652.

[32]Diane Ravitch, *The Schools We Deserve* (New York: Basic Books, 1985), p. 34.

[34]Provincial Committee on Aims and Objectives in the Schools of Ontario, *Living and Learning* (Toronto: Ontario Department of Education, 1968), p. 55.

Response

Michael J. B. Jackson

The key to Donald Wilson's paper is the recognition that the state has taken over a function, the education of children, which was not originally its own. Thus, the state, perhaps representing the society, gets to impose some of its own values on education. I say that this recognition of the role of the state is the key to Wilson's account because from it follow his three themes: progress, state authority, and the reform of educational practice.

But let us begin with a caveat. It is perhaps significant that we would talk of a state *education* system but not so readily (although we can think of exceptions) of the state's being responsible for the *up-bringing* of children, and conversely of parents as bringing their children up but not so readily as educating them (although here again we can think of occasions when we would want to say this). The state may have taken over responsibility for education, but we still seem to have an intuitive sense of an acceptable sort of distinction between different parts of a child's upbringing — one part belonging to the state, the other to the child's parents. So a child's education is an ambiguous topic; and perhaps we will decide that only one part of it is the proper preserve of the state (outside Plato's Republic, that is) or at least that some part of it is not well expressed in terms of the concerns of the state. And it is this latter claim which is my first thesis.

Progress

Wilson has chosen to focus his paper on the concept of progress in our history of public education — an idea every bit as important historically in the educational ideology of our southern neighbour, the United States. This progress has been an accepted value among educational theorists, teachers, administrators, and critics alike; and even today parents, who may well wonder about the state of education generally, often report that their own children are getting a good education in their local school. Or at least this has seemed to us to be the case until recently: Wilson has reminded us of

Bercuson, Bothwell, and Granatstein. And, for a parallel, one only has to think of how critical reports on public education have been in the U.S. of late — even suggesting that if the damage done to the education system could be traced to a foreign power, one might well talk of war, sabotage, or treason.

But all these doubts suggest that Wilson is still right to focus on the idea of progress: critics and defenders alike share this commitment, and the criticisms and alleged failures suggest its traditional centrality and a continuing faith as much as its present dubiety. Each critic may view the status quo as a disaster but that is because education has failed to achieve its promise, and each time there is proposed a panacea which will deliver the promise of education — the progress we seek. Proponents of the status quo believe in educational progress, and so do its critics; nobody believes it has been achieved, but everybody thinks it can be. In my view, *these panaceas are the crux of the problem*, but perhaps not for the reasons we or their proponents might think. And this is my second thesis.

But again we must pause. Is the recent questioning of educational progress and the present quality of education in our schools all that new? I suggest not. Hilda Neatby's *So Little for the Mind* long predates *The Great Brain Robbery*. And the same has been true in the United States: one might look back to the curriculum reforms of the 1890s, but there are more recent examples in the purported failures of progressive education or the education-for-life movement, and in the promised remedies of the academic rigour of the post-Sputnik era or the back-to-the-basics ideology.

So, we have always believed in this value of progress in public education, and we have always felt somehow that it has not yet been achieved, but what is it? What do we now think constitutes educational progress, and are our conceptions now so different from those of earlier times? Could it be a nebulous, empty 'will-o'-the-wisp'? And could that be why we never achieve it? Or is there something new today which gives us a different problem? Or has there been an on-going problem?

State Authority

There is a second key theme in Wilson's paper, equally fascinating and ambiguous: the role of the state. Wilson rightly talks of the rise of public schooling, of state supported mass education, of schools which will socialize immigrants to the national ideology, culture, and way of living, and of the use of schools to promote national goals and values. We can hardly be surprised when education is classed together with manpower training or when universities are placed under departments of career development. We may cringe and sense that there is a difference; but where, in Wilson's view, can there any longer be the distinction which he implies between the state and its schools?

Here there lurks an ambiguity, I suggest, in Wilson's account of the role of the state. As the school system becomes synonymous with education, the state *replaces* the home and the church, he says, but that state influence is still *filtered* through the school and the church. As education and public schooling become increasingly identified and as government supported provincial school systems develop, Wilson tells us, it is *the school and the church, not the state*, which become the central agents for social improvement and for intellectual and moral guidance — whether the goals be intended or unintended, conscious or unconscious, and even in matters of civics and citizenship. Some distinction remains.

Real school reforms then do become pragmatic, and neither state nor church nor parental values gain the day. In this sense, the OECD report is right: education in Canada is not politicized. This brings us back to my first thesis — that educational concerns are not always well expressed in terms of the concerns of the state.

Reform

From a discussion of progress we come to a third theme — educational reform— well illustrated in Wilson's paper, and there seems here too to be a truth as clear in American education as in our own: what the schools have been criticized for doing or failing to do has traditionally borne no relation to actual practices in them. Reformers presumably lament, for example, that progressive education was never really implemented and therefore never really given a trial; their critics attack not educational realities but an ideology which they abhor. Our own Science Council found it useful in its recent report, *Science for Every Student*, to distinguish between the stated curriculum and the actual curriculum. The literature on educational change is replete with admonitions that enunciating and mandating policy changes do little to alter practices, and attempts are made at explaining why this might be so.

Some have even suggested that it might be a good thing that teacher practices are not simply a matter of implementing a stated policy: schools are protected in this way from ill-considered and fleeting programs of social and educational reform dreamt up by those entirely outside the business of teaching, and the traditional wisdom and experience of teachers (their practical rationality) is given some scope.

But if the focus of the attacks on education is not actually the educational practices at all, then should we not wonder if their real aim is not also something else? Have two distinct things become confused? Again, we come back to my second thesis: what do we understand by that educational progress whose achievement would constitute reform?

Wilson's Thesis

Now, if I have rightly identified the three themes in Wilson's paper, we have something of a muddle. Critics and educational reformers as well as apologists for the status quo have always agreed on the value of educational progress though not, obviously, on the value of what they think is being done in schools. But, it turns out, what they have actually been debating is ideology and not educational practice at all. And, in any case, the relationship between the state and its schools is an ambiguous one. No wonder the debates seem pointless and what reforms exist are merely pragmatic ones. And, since progress is a concept in need of further specification, the problem then *appears* to Wilson to be a lack of consensus about goals — about what progress is — and, as Wilson suggests, this is just what you would expect in a society which lacks a clearly defined set of shared beliefs.

What then is progress in general, and in particular what would progress be in education? Within the school, it seems, progress has frequently meant material progress, the provision of more and better resources. (It has probably also taken the form of more and better educated teachers.) In society, progress seems to have been associated with economic concerns, with the production of wealth and with the provision of a qualified and employed labour-force, technological advantage, and reduced unemployment and crime especially among the young. But these *are* shared values, and it is Wilson who believes that the problem today is the *lack* of a common system of beliefs (and presumably a shared set of values).

Besides, the competition of values and systems of beliefs cannot be a new problem. Our society may be more tolerant of a plurality of beliefs and practices, but socializing the immigrants (who might bring with them foreign idedogies and values) and teaching the lower classes (who might otherwise become rebellious) the right values (their place, and the importance of hard and diligent work) were social and educational policies which made sense only in the face of competing systems of beliefs and values. The plurality of beliefs which underlies Wilson's critique of educational progress is not new either.

So what exactly does Wilson's thesis about progress come to? It seems to me that he should be looking more closely at the content of those educational objectives which he rightly identifies as the crux of the problem. Progress, of course, is a value on which almost everybody can agree precisely because it is vacuous without further specification. But, as Wilson has argued, those objectives rarely relate to real educational practice. To boot, as I have argued, the relationship between the state and its schools is neither a clear or simple one.

Michael J.B. Jackson

Educational Objectives

When we look again at the kinds of objectives which the state wishes to have for its schools, we find they are often matters over which the schools have relatively little control: employment, industrial strategies, and economic cycles are not useful terms in which to express educational objectives. When the state takes over responsibility for the education of children, then it does get to impose some of its own goals, but its proper goals (security and the well-being of its citizens) are only indirectly related to education. And this, I suggest, is where the problem lies. Progress for the state in the achievement of its goals is not essentially educational progress; and educational progress is only tangentially of interest to the state, as any other of its functions should serve the interests of its citizens. What we have is a confusion of *specific educational* and *general social* goals. Outside Plato's Republic, pursuit of the one is not likely to coincide with pursuit of the other.

It may be useful too to return for a moment to our original caveat, that state education is only part of a child's up-bringing. The question to be asked is surely: what is the legitimate interest of the state in that child's education or up-bringing? Our conceptions of education and the state are not those of Plato. What we need, I would suggest, is a realistic set of genuinely *educational* objectives, objectives which it is within our power to realize.

It may be tempting to seek funding for our schools and universities by offering to address a whole range of social and politically fashionable goals, but this is a recipe for disaster: for one thing, it is beyond our power to achieve goals which are outside our control, and so we lose credibility, and, for another, we destroy our own mission by distorting our educational priorities. But this is what we are driven to do because we find ourselves in need of money (which we would wisely spend on worthwhile educational ends), and we promise what we must to get the support that we need. This distorts our own educational institutions (making research, technology, an industrial strategy, employment or whatever, artificially important) and it does so to their own internal disadvantage. And it makes us promise what we can never deliver because what we must promise distorts our own educational role — and this we do to our external disadvantage.

2 Half a League, Half a Lunge, Half a Loaf Onward, All In the Valley of the Shadow of Silicon: Canadian Public Education and Society Since 1970

Hugh A. Stevenson

Introduction

To focus your attention quickly on the major characteristics of Canadian public education since 1970, the title of my assessment deliberately parodies the unlikely combination of Tennyson's romantic tribute to *The Charge of the Light Brigade*, the *Twenty-Third Psalm* and the biblical geographic location of the shadow of death and more recently, the silicon chip. The metaphoric parallels should not be taken too literally, allowing for reasonable hyperbole. There are, however, some striking similarities among these strange bedfellows that illustrate the Canadian experience with public education and that, I hope, will provide you with an enticing basis for further discussion and debate.

Like the Crimean War for Britain between 1854 and 1856, Canadian public education in the 1970s and 1980s was driven by complex national and international conditions as well as competing economic, social, professional and political forces. The accumulation of key, essentially practical accomplishments of nation-building (in one case a world-class navy and in the other an impressive educational infrastructure) made participation in the exciting enterprises of each time period possible. This potential fueled adventurous public aspirations to exploit new technologies to speed communications via the Suez and the stratosphere respectively and to compete commercially for new wealth and all sorts of heightened gratification.

In each case, the stakes were high, involving the future well-being of millions, ominously in the case of failure, positively in the case of victory but uncertainly overall. Hard times prevailed making public funds scarce; both periods historically witnessed the clamour of competing public priorities for their use; the din influenced decision-making, spreading the available resources too thinly in some sectors and circumstances tended to encourage privatization. Like the conduct of the war, the delivery of public education came to be directed exclusively in essential areas by politicians, their power often selectively ill-informed and influenced rather predictably more by public opinion than professional insight and experience.

As the war dragged on, the public's faith in education eroded noticeably; criticism of its conduct escalated with assistance from the press awakened by marketable horror stories, arm chair rumblings of misman-agement and failures among the accused to produce convincing evidence of success. In the classrooms and laboratories at the front where many less than ideal conditions prevailed, there seemed to be considerable confusion about objectives in some quarters; the chain of command became politi-cized and advocacy groups formed lobbies for both public and self-interested causes. 'Big Guns' sat comically and no doubt uncomfortably side by side in the anterooms of legislative committees waiting their turn to seek 'Big Bucks' for similarly virtuous but competing causes.[1]

Communications often failed and many overtures to produce coopera-tive efforts proved to be more frustrating than fruitful for everyone. Facilities and equipment (new twenty or thirty years earlier) were expected to do service without adequate refurbishment. Once reliable technologies of horse, rider and sabre, the army's texts, teachers and chalk were pitted unrealistically against the superior technology of entrenched Cossack cannon firing on three sides with an equivalent power to the more contemporary blast of the information explosion and the plastic and glass encased artillery of the computer-communications revolution.

The army aged rapidly as experience brought disillusionment and despair, replacing the youthful optimism and thoughts of adventure and glory that had filled soldiers' minds as they marched aboard troop ships. A somewhat similar mood shift is often now reported among educators, bloodied by the stress of modern public education at all levels, underfunded and confronted incessantly as they are by the requirement to do more with less. While some would wish the opportunity to serve indefinitely, retire-ment is a close enough option for others to offer the attractive prospect of welcome relief. For various reasons recruitment came to be an important priority in both cases and in one, the problem was made worse by an existing drain of some with training who opted to soldier for competing international powers.

Finally, just as The Light Brigade knew its fate as soon as the order was given to advance, Canadian public educators also knew what lay before them early in the 1970s when the orders for funding ceilings, accountability, behavioural objectives, declining enrolments, new services, accessibility and a more conservative curriculum were issued. The cavalry did its duty without question; educators did theirs differently by cooperat-ing with public enquiries, enunciating warnings, pointing out alternatives and consequences, protecting themselves in the clinches, learning the fine points of politics and the basic lesson of the need to inform public opinion. The immediate result in both cases was pretty much the same. Both groups rode gallantly into the valley. Both experienced the shot and shell of the cannonade. Both rode out again diminished by the experience.

The 21st Lancers, however, retired from the field, the folly of their sacrifice to a lost cause to be immortalized by the Bard. Public educators had no such merciful choice since their cause was not lost so irrevocably. Their role historically is to re-group, renew their ranks and to return to the conflict time after time rallying around new banners such as special education, more funds for research, French immersion, early childhood education, salvation for arts education, better teacher education, renewed efforts in science and mathematics education, more effective reading and writing programs, the need for heritage language courses, life skills, computer literacy, adult and continuing and distance education initiatives and, most recently, the prevention of deadly AIDS through better education.

At this point the analogy must come to an end. We know the results of the tragic Crimean War. It led to reforms of all kinds in the British army, the government and, of course, hospital care. As well, public opinion achieved new levels of respect in the continuing evolution of democracy and politically motivated enterprises. The outcome of the similarly ill-fated battle of Canadian public education since 1970 is, of course, not yet completely known. We do know, however, that improvements in health care have been achieved at the expense of other essential social services. Also more people understand that the conflict of the last eighteen years is part of an on-going war where no end is in sight; one where genuine advances come very slowly and gains and losses take a long time to assess. The pain and debilitation of an inadequate education takes years to be felt with the same intensity as other chronic diseases, and there is no known cure or effective palliative comfort for the ailment. There is not much in light of our recent educational history and present embattled circumstances to make one optimistic about public education's immediate prospects. One may hope, however, that this period in Canada's education will be remembered historically for more innovative accomplishments than the enlightened leadership of the Crimean War that gave us the raglan sleeve and the cardigan sweater.

Essential Background Considerations

Before I turn to the third section of my paper where the present scene in Canadian public education is described in relation to central social and economic concerns, I would like to draw on one more well-known literary figure and make three summary observations that I think are essential as background to understanding the central theme.

While I was preparing this paper, I came upon a comparative description of what it is to be a Canadian by Robertson Davies. I liked it instantly because it told me a good deal about our national identity, the essential nature of some public processes like education and, perhaps most importantly, 'how' and 'when' and 'why' we go about changing fundamental aspects of our society. He feels, rightly I think, that Canadians are a 'cold, lost and lonely race, neither American nor British, but tougher and funnier than either nation realizes' and that 'the lash of necessity has made us a nation of thrivers'.[2]

Once again the quality of our thriving is now the central issue that confronts the nation. The extent to which public education has the capacity to contribute positively is perceived to be considerable in general terms. There is no longer much agreement, however, on specifics, a deficiency which places the entire enterprise in doubt and the outcome very much in jeopardy. Whatever happens, Canadian educators are now forced to play 'catch-up' while dealing with an increasingly sceptical, angry and fearful society.

Three other background observations for consideration are:

(a) All of us are guilty of speaking and thinking falsely and unrealistically about Canadian public education. I am as guilty as the rest and I have just done it again in the preceding sentence. Constitutionally, there is no such thing as 'Canadian public education'. Also, we all think of 'systems' when in reality all that exists are provincial educational sectors at various levels that should function as integrated, inter-related systems. Occasionally some sectors do but not often enough to be called 'systems'. Similarly, while the public and some politicians have no difficulty with the concept, virtually all levels of education in Canada are public. Many educators, however, seldom see themselves that way and universities, even with acknowledged safeguards for academic freedom, are the worst offenders. If this situation is not 'funny' in the sense that Robertson Davies intended it, one must admit that at the least our behaviour is a bit peculiar.

While public education receives a great deal of attention in this society, perhaps because it operates in discrete sectors, we tend to underestimate its size, complexity and the nature of its contributions.[3] We are prone to forget that we are committed publicly to mass education at wide-ranging and all-inclusive age levels by overly concentrating on the benefits purportedly accruing to the individual (or vice versa if the argument fits better). Several important things get lost in these discussions — the limits that reality imposes on our universal commitment to equalizing educational opportunity, just how much success educationally is directly dependent on the responsibility that is accepted by individuals and their families, and how many are in a position to accept this responsibility in relation to their personal ability and familial circumstances.

(b) The real relationship that now exists and perhaps always has existed between education and work is not very well understood. Most of the driving forces are beyond the control of either individuals or educators but there can be little doubt that however we have understood work in relation to life's passage in the past, its nature is now changing rapidly and fundamentally. The recently revived recognition for the market value of a sound general education evident in several educational sectors may provide a clue to the likely direction of some curriculum reforms in the future. Finally, in these respects we tend to forget that Canada is not alone in the problems that we face educationally and that by world standards (including the Pacific rim experience) the potential of what we have to offer is considerable.

(c) As background, since 1970 it appears that public education has been the subject of more varied and more intense criticism than at any other time in our history. Perhaps it is simply a phenomenon of the information age, generally stressful times, or a sign that education in Canada has come of age recently with the completion of its college sectors and tangible recognition for the needs of adults? We seldom consider how young some sectors and services are and the time that it takes for them to contribute fully in a rapidly changing world.[4] The causes of the criticism are undoubtedly more complex and their consequences are obviously damaging. The point is that we often know too little about public education to respond effectively, creating a situation where it is impossible to identify legitimate problems, judge their magnitude and remedy them. To me, that kind of situation is very dangerous for any public enterprise.

In several ways I have intended these general observations to indicate the extent to which public educators are 'lost' and 'lonely' and to allude to possible directions for some of our 'thriving' prompted by 'necessity'. It remains to be seen how 'tough' we are.

Canadian Society and Public Education in the mid-80s: The Differences Since 1970

Whether or not the quality of education has improved since 1970 is not the real issue. It has improved in many demonstrable ways in a period of Canadian history fraught with difficulties and increasing demands from the public for educational services. Whether Canadian public education has been improved sufficiently and how it should be improved further in relation to national and global, social and economic conditions is a more appropriate focus for any current reassessment.

In many ways at all levels, public education is better than it was eighteen years ago. While much remains to be done, public education has adjusted to large shifts in enrolment driven by demographic factors and the perceived preferences of students. It now serves more people of different ages, caters better to exceptionalities, and adjustments are underway responding to the pluralistic and multicultural realities of Canadian life. The institutions are tougher, leaner, more sophisticated, more political, more aware, and more realistic.

Making the Match published in 1986 by the Corporate Higher Education Forum should have put to rest most fears that large numbers of university graduates are not meeting the general employment needs of Canadian corporations. Colleges report acceptably high levels of employment among their graduates. Secondary schools generally sustain high retention rates but they experience difficulty maintaining them and their dropouts undoubtedly contribute to the overall difficulty of youth unemployment. By comparison, however, to lower levels in Europe or Canadian standards early in the 1970s, very high levels of accessibility have been achieved overall.

In relation to Canada's continued commitment to the ideal of equal educational opportunity, most criticisms that quality of delivery and discipline have slipped dangerously have simply not been documented convincingly. It is far too easy to make education the scapegoat for failure to meet the unchecked demands that elements of society heap upon it. The messages that public education cannot be expected to respond to all social problems, that successful educational changes can only be accomplished slowly, and that the bond between education and employment is only one link in a long chain, are ones that many citizens and politicians have never wanted to comprehend.

Educational sectors, however, have been rationalized to the bone and in some cases into the bone, leaving schools, colleges and universities struggling to preserve standards. Those who long for the purportedly clear measures of quality of our yesteryear of elitism and exclusiveness delude themselves in fantasies of province-wide examinations, the screening successes of admissions tests, the evils of grade inflation and obligations only to the brightest and the best. They have misread history and the realities of contemporary society. They rarely consider phenomena such as 'teaching to the test', the pedagogic influence of machine-marked examinations, the massive logistic problems of administering provincial tests or the lack of historical results for comparative purposes.[5] Those who insist on having it both ways in the educational mix of openness and excellence will always be disillusioned.

Among the significant differences since 1970 is the greater urgency of Canada's education-related problems and an emerging climate of recognition by many sectors of society demanding action involving much more than continued sustaining efforts to keep public education alive. The focus of this complaining is now aimed squarely at governments, school boards and teachers, and there appears to be a new bite and bitterness to both informed and ignorant recent critical articulations of the difficulties supporting the argument for urgency.

In their third annual poll *Maclean's* recently reported 'a volatile national mood that mingles optimism and uncertainty, idealism and a new pragmatism'[6] and they did not ask any questions about public education. There was, however, no shortage of educational commentary in the press and the professional literature.

Late in 1986 the Canadian Bureau of International Education published *Closing the Doors?*[7] which illustrates vividly how badly Canada compares to other nations in our ability to attract international students and how badly government policy has blundered. In a special Winter 1986–87 issue dealing with 'Global Education' (all that international, global village, war and peace stuff in the curriculum) *The History and Social Science Teacher* reported that Canadian teachers use a wide variety of materials but that 'research on global education in Canada is almost non-existent'.[8] *Interchange* carried reviews of books with titles like *Education Under Siege* wherein the reviewer hung his position arguably around his contention that 'for political as well as logical reasons — education needs to be taken seriously in its own right if it's to flourish'.[9] Mark Holmes in an article entitled 'The Educational Establishment — The People's Master ...' courageously tackled the unresolved serious issues of how well reading and writing are taught in Ontario and how research is abused by nearly everyone. His secondary theme, however, notes the very real dangers that have developed because of a 'serious gap between the preferred educational directions of the educational establishment (who hold the power politically) and those of the public-at-large' whose wishes go unheeded.[10]

In January 1987 *The Toronto Star* put 'Education: Back in the Hot Seat' arguing 'that the standard of education ... will be front and centre when Ontario next goes to the polls' because 'The millions poured into separate school funding had the effect of lifting the lid off public expectations about what needs to be done in our schools'.[11] Two days later, *The Toronto Sun* ran an article entitled 'Wasted Teaching Time — Spotlight's on Bad Schooling' dealing with the birth of a group calling itself The Council for Excellence in Education (CEE) whose 'main mandate is based on the idea that "public education is too important to be left as the preserve of politicized boards and educational bureaucracies"'. A spokesperson for the CEE claimed, without any supporting evidence, that 'In Canada, one out of every 10 students has a learning disability, and 50% of them have acquired it through the school systems'. The same piece touted one of 'the brave among our university professors' who 'have been sounding the alarm bells on public education for years to no avail' for an article he wrote reporting the results of a 'trivia' quiz taken by some of his university students published in February 1987 by *Toronto Life*.[12] You will not be astonished to learn that everyone does not know that Quasimodo did not write *For Whom the Bell Tolls*. You will not, however, learn very much that is generalizable about the quality of public education in Canada.

In January 1987, the Ontario Federation of Students called for the federal government to 'develop a long-term policy aimed at ending discriminatory practices that discourage foreign students from studying in Canadian colleges and universities', one more rock in the avalanche of objection that has been heaped on governments since differential fees were imposed in seven Canadian provinces over the virtually unanimous objection of educators at all levels. At the same time the Canadian Federation of Students staged a national week of action around protest and lobbying aimed at the federal and provincial governments to support their claim that there is a broadly based 'crisis' in post-secondary education.[13]

Some of the harshest and most ominous criticism from observers such as Walter Light, Chief Executive Officer of Northern Telecom, The Science Council of Canada and others has been collected together in a new book on community colleges. We face a 'crippling shortage in almost every body of knowledge' that Canada will need in the next twenty years, a period when we may not survive 'as a modern viable, international industrial power in the Information Age'. Our productivity, competitiveness, ability to attract investment, our capacity for research and development are either dismal or weak to the point that 'our cultural and political sovereignty' may 'be permanently jeopardized'. 'Conflict rather than agreement and cooperation is the standard approach to settling priorities.' Youth unemployment is very serious, constituting an extremely politically volatile group. 'Even the prospect of a "techno-peasant" class in Canada cannot be ruled out.' We are told that 'Canadians need to gird themselves for the prospect of living in a society in which anything approaching national consensus on any significant issue will be extraordinarily difficult. . . . There is no universally suitable choice of action. . . . All the issues call for fresh vision, anticipation and change'.[14]

Since the spring of 1986, the Canadian Teachers' Federation (CTF) has been engaged in an extensive survey that apart from issues related to teaching and other genuine educational matters attempts to examine the nature of stresses imposed on the schools and students by society — ones that reflect the concerns of parents, teachers, children and adolescents resulting from changes that schools and educators must cope with although they are not equipped to do so. The organization has targeted: the increasing socialization of children 'by the media and their peers rather than by adults, . . . the use of drugs, including alcohol . . ., sexual abuse and neglect of children . . .', the inadequacy of 'out-of-school and pre-school child care . . ., a society unwilling to accommodate new family forms . . ., childhood depression, despair and suicide . . . [which are] becoming more common . . ., widespread . . . hopelessness about the possibility of employment . . ., unrealistic and damaging expectations of self and others' due to 'intense role-orientation by gender, . . . the powerlessness of young people in the face of nuclear terror . . . reflected in their lack of willingness to plan for their own lives or [to] become active in social change issues'.[15]

The CTF feels that 'the urgency of the need to reconcile the goals and practices of education with the challenges of our emerging social context . . . is unique. . . . [They] believe public education in Canada is at a turning point'. The organization representing 290,000 elementary and secondary teachers sees these issues as part of a 'new agenda' they want resolved through better social and educational policies. At the same time the Canadian Education Association has renewed its long-standing efforts to improve 'public understanding and support' for schools. And, the Council of Ministers of Education, Canada (CMEC) noted a number of these same concerns in its 1986 report to The International Conference on Education in Geneva.[16]

Politicians generally and particularly those from parties in power have tended not to be either constructively critical of education or very fretful about quality. Both issues are difficult to substantiate and to do so would invite counter criticism regarding government accountability and the sort of media coverage that is unwelcome. They have, however, fought among themselves publicly, within the CMEC, across party lines and levels of government and weighed competing social priorities. Seldom have they been as responsive as educational critics and advisors have recommended. The bite of bitterness and disillusionment is perhaps most evident on the west coast at the moment but other examples in recent years are not difficult to find elsewhere.[17]

In future this sort of confrontation may prove to be helpful if it provokes more appropriate political responses but it has not done so in the past and the tactic is socially expensive. It damages confidence among the citizenry for both educators and politicians and is likely to become more legalistic as the Charter of Rights and Freedoms becomes a last constitutional court of appeal to resolve educational problems. 'The nature of political action in Canada . . . [could change] from one of lobbying elected legislators to that of proceeding with a panoply of legal experts to seek redress through the courts.'[18] These prospects worry everyone who knows about them. Recently in the first major educational test case under the Charter the Supreme Court ruled in favour of full funding for Ontario's Roman Catholic Separate Schools. How far away can test cases on educational malpractice be?

As well, finances and levels of funding, constant sources of concern throughout the entire period, have reached a ridiculous stage. It seems to be impossible to determine real per-pupil costs and expenditures and to know if they are rising or falling when governments use at least thirteen different sets of books and provinces refuse to open their books to provide essential data or to be accountable for the use of federal transfer funds designated for education.[19] These issues have plagued Established Programs Financing (EPF) negotiations for years and are very symptomatic of another central difficulty in resolving our educational concerns regarding quality and the solutions to social and economic policy questions. Too often, 'in this country, we are too prone to be parochial in our educational concerns and stances, both in the sense of being oriented to single issues and single models and in our regionalism.'[20] We obfuscate broader issues and the fact that we are caught up in a world crisis that is economic, scientific, technological and social as well as educational. Our political partisanship, our regionalism, and our fascination with the localized details of finance has often caused us to stray from the real point of the overarching problems or to unite sufficiently to confront them appropriately.

The results of two recent research studies have the potential to set political and educational sectors off again on narrowly conceived paper chases that could further distract all of us from more important, comprehensive objectives. Economist David K. Foot has demonstrated rather convincingly that political responses to youth unemployment in Canada have been incorrectly targeted to the wrong age cohort. Two other economists from the Université de Montréal seem to have proven that 'tuition fees could be increased in all regions of Canada' without affecting the high demand for 'university schooling' and provincial governments might 'reduce their subsidies to universities'.[21] One can only hope that these interesting conclusions do not lead us into another decade of debate concerning the reality of underfunding and who pays, wherein quality considerations and priority-setting become lost in retrogressive verbiage interpreting multiple balance sheets when the real issue is political responsiveness.[22]

By comparison to the actions of many elected officials, the contributions of Canadian educators since 1970, particularly their critical insights and their protectiveness of quality, should bring colour to political cheeks.[23] While not perfect and always virtuous, the behaviour of educators has been a highly responsible professional and social activity, very different from earlier periods in the '50s and most of the '60s when a Canadian-made critical product was nearly non-existent. Then with the exception of Hilda Neatby in 1953 and Jean-Paul Desbiens in 1960 who offended many Canadian educators, or Frank MacKinnon who was early in recognizing the political potential of public education, the harshest educational voices that prodded public and political awareness were American and British; the other forces that combined to produce an unprecedented response educationally in the 1960s were the practical ones of educating thousands of children, a type of unemployment and labour shortage recognized late in the 1950s that it was felt could be met by the traditional vocationalism of schools and international scientific and technological forces that made the required huge public expenditures acceptable.

A somewhat similar set of forces has emerged now to confront Canadians but with several differences. Canadian educators understand them better and they have played a front-running part in alerting public opinion. We know the issues and they are remarkably similar but vastly more complex. The four most important differences, all products of the '70s and '80s, are: the overall ungovernability of the educational enterprise; the excessive politicization that has introduced new levels of confrontation and frozen our ability to make progress; the difficulty of responding to criticism effectively and halting the erosion of public confidence; the massiveness of our public education at all levels wherein sectors compete rather than cooperate and fail to communicate effectively to recognize common problems and seek comprehensive solutions to them.

These are the most serious developments that bring the quality of Canadian public education into question; until progress is made in resolving them, the contemporary and future quality of life for everyone who lives in this country will be compromised. Canada rather desperately needs to get its educational and political acts together before the nation is left behind in a fast-moving world where the laggards court epithets of irrelevance and public disdain.

Since the early '70s the momentum for more recognition and direct involvement of the federal government in education at all levels in a variety of ways particularly related to funding, development of policy, the establishment of priorities and improved inter-governmental relations has been a persistent theme in the educational literature and the agendas of national agencies such as the AUCC the CMEC and others. Argument tends to focus on the need for greater federal government involvement and funding for research and post-secondary sectors, however, elementary and secondary education are involved too because of sound economic analysis and common sense.[24] Allan Sharp put it very nicely in the February 1987 issue of the *CAUT Bulletin*:

> If we are going to survive in the world economy, our needs are very clear. We need more research to fuel innovation and invention and more researchers to understand the information explosion and to extract from it what is relevant to Canada. We need a well educated population with well developed critical faculties capable of innovation, of coping with rapid change, as well as of maintaining the requisite social perspective to ensure that technology is our servant and not our master.[25]

His arguments were meant as a rationale for his conclusion that: 'The need for a vibrant university system to help us achieve these goals has never been greater.' Obviously, however, that is not going to be enough. Elementary and secondary schools, and post-secondary colleges must be included to achieve his desired mix of economic advantages and social stability sustained by a sufficiently 'well-educated population'. Also, adult education and job re-training have been involved in this quest since the late '60s and now the mood in that generally polite segment of our educative society shows elements of rising anger against inappropriate 'quick fix' measures such as the National Training Act designed to train people for emerging 'high-tech' jobs. The Director of the Extension Department at St. Francis Xavier University and Chairperson of the Cape Breton Development Corporation now asks: 'Should we be part of a hoax that we are training for jobs, when there are no jobs?'[26]

Actual progress towards more recognition and a more realistic role for the federal government has been slow, but persistent. Nay-sayers, the politically timid, and the advocates of the status quo have held the field for too long and for plainly unrealistic reasons.[27] The depth of Canada's socio-educational and economic difficulties has become more demanding of new levels of political cooperation. The concept of a national office of education has been bandied about over the last two decades (actually since the 1890s) and very recently.[28] In October 1987 over 500 invited representatives of governments, education, labour and Canadian business joined forces to hold a National Forum on Post Secondary Education.[29] Also, the CMEC has agreed on a set of limited 'principles' to guide their future dealings with the federal government and that educational policies for foreign students are 'confusing' and 'ultimately detrimental to Canada'.[30] To these recent developments one can add the rising voices in favour of a higher national priority for education and more federal involvement that are heard from leaders in industry, the positive work of the Corporate Higher Education Forum, and the periodic editorial support these initiatives receive from the press.[31] No longer is the federal government seen as the only source of essential funding as more universities turn to the private sector just as other levels of education tend to be doing to develop co-operative programs and projects.

A co-operative coalition among educators and private sector interests seems to have begun to gel, demanding constructive national responses to genuinely Canadian social, economic and educational difficulties. The thrust of the argumentation is squarely focused on more immediate responsiveness from political sectors — neither advocating nor expecting instant solutions — requiring comprehensive, forthright action without further delay in the best interests of the nation.

Although much more remains to be done, particularly to improve communication and co-operation among the several sectors of public education, the historical record, the available contemporary evidence and opinion force me to conclude on a mixed note of optimism that may be more hopeful than real and an element of pessimism that may be more real than hopeful.

The confluence of forces taking shape now once existed but was lost in Canada by 1970. It has not existed since the years immediately preceding and following 1960 when Canadians awakened nationally and found timely solutions to the economic and educational problems of the day.[32] The same sort of awakening seems to be taking place now. I am hopeful that it will continue and will revive three things Canadians have not put together as a working coalition for many years '— a firm faith in the value of public education, belief that we could achieve fundamental reforms to meet rapidly changing circumstances, and a national dimension to our concerns'.[33] Canadians appear to 'thrive' best when they must; the signs are that the time has come again to demonstrate this salient feature of our national character before we become a colder, more lost and lonelier race because of our inability to work together effectively, another well-known and pessimistic characteristic of our Canadianism. Ultimately, I am hopeful that, if not for better reasons this time, the sting of Robertson Davies' 'lash of necessity' will work for Canada once again.

There is, however, one serious flaw in the current promising beginning that has been made towards a revived national consensus. It is too narrowly conceived to be totally successful. Its main objective presently is an enhanced research capacity to improve economic competitiveness in only one admittedly very significant sector — the complex high-tech computer-communications industry. These needs are undoubtedly important and they must be met. The overriding issue, however, is to improve the quality and comprehensiveness of public education in *all* areas, restoring high levels of consensus and confidence in a truly national enterprise which intimately involves the future prospects of the entire citizenry. The lesson of the '70s and '80s is surely that proceeding further educationally by advances of 'Half a League, Half a Lunge, Half a Loaf Onward' will not work to anyone's long-term advantage.

Notes

[1] Gordon Sanderson, 'Education System's Big Guns Seek Big Bucks,' *The London Free Press*, February 20, 1987, p. A8.

[2] 'Canada Not So Dry', *The Daily Telegraph*, October 11, 1986, p. 14.

[3] Canadian Education Association, *The CEA Handbook* (Toronto: CEA, 1986); Association of Universities and Colleges of Canada, *Directory of Canadian Universities* (Ottawa: AUCC, 1986) and T.J. Wuester, 'The Harmonization of School Legislation in Canada,' in R.C.C. Cuming (ed.), *Perspectives on the Harmonization of Law in Canada* (Toronto: University of Toronto Press, 1985), p. 154 and Organization for Economic Co-operation and Development. *Review of National Policies for Education — Canada* (Paris: OECD, 1976).

[4] B.Y. Card, 'A State of Sociology of Education in Canada — A Further Look,' *Canadian Journal of Education*, vol. I no. 4 (1976), pp. 3–32; Patrick J. Harrington, 'A Comparative Perspective on Recent Trends in the History of Education in Canada,' *History of Education Quarterly*, vol. 26 no. 1 (1986), pp. 71–86; *Curriculum Inquiry* began publication in 1970; *Interchange* in 1969; M.J.B. Jackson, 'Three Decades,' *The Study of Education: Canada, 1982* (Edmonton: Canadian Society for the Study of Education, 1982) and Ian Winchester, Mark Holmes, and Hugh Oliver (eds.),

'Illuminating Education: The Uses of Science, History, and Philosophy in Educational Thought,' *Interchange*, vol. 17 no. 2 (1986), special issue.

[5]For example: D.J. Bercuson, R. Bothwell, and J.L. Granatstein, *The Great Brain Robbery: Canada's Universities on the Road to Ruin* (Toronto: McClelland and Stewart, 1984).

[6]*Maclean's*, vol. 100 no. 1, (January 5, 1987), pp. 1, 24–74.

[7]Canadian Bureau of International Education, *Closing the Doors? A Statistical Report on International Students in Canada 1983–85* (Ottawa: CBIE, 1986).

[8]*The History and Social Science Teacher*, vol. 22 no. 2 (Winter 1986–87), p. 71.

[9]*Interchange*, vol. 17 no. 4 (1986), pp. 100–101.

[10]Mark Holmes, 'The Educational Establishment — The People's Master: The Case of English Education in Ontario,' *Education Canada*, vol. 26 no. 4, (1986), p. 30.

[11]Rosemary Speirs, 'Education: Back in the Hot Seat Again,' *The Toronto Star*, January 24, 1987, n.p.

[12]Judy McLeod, 'Wasted Teaching Time: Spotlight's on Bad Schooling,' *The Toronto Sun*, January 26, 1987, n.p. and Alberto Manguel, 'Quasimodo Wrote *For Whom The Bell Tolls*: True or False?' *Toronto Life*, February 1987.

[13]*The London Free Press*, January 24, 1987, p. A9.

[14]John D. Dennison and P. Gallagher, *Canada's Community Colleges: A Critical Analysis* (Vancouver: UBC Press, 1986), pp. 133–40.

[15]Frank Garritty (President of the CTF) to H.A. Stevenson April 10, 1986 and enclosed survey papers. See also: Special Senate Committee on Youth, *Youth: A Plan of Action* (Ottawa: Senate of Canada, 1986).

[16]*Ibid.*, and Canadian Education Association, *Marketing The School System: Building Public Confidence in Schools* (Toronto: CEA, 1986), p. 63 and Council of Ministers of Education, Canada, *Education in Canada 1984–1986 Report to the 40th Session, International Conference on Education, Geneva* (Toronto: CMEC, 1986), pp. 19–20.

[17]C. Kilian, *School Wars: The Assault on B.C. Education* (Vancouver: New Star Books, 1985) and virtually any recent publication discussing education at any level in British Columbia. See also: T. Fleming, 'Restraints, Reform, and Reallocation,' *Education Canada*, vol. 25 no. 1, (1985), pp. 4–11.

[18]A.R. Wells, 'The Educational Significance of Canada's Constitution,' *Education Canada*, vol. 25 no. 2, (1985), p. 37; M.E. Manley-Casimir and T.R. Sussel, 'The Equality Provisions of the Canadian Charter of Rights and Educational Policy: Preparations for Implementation,' *Interchange*, vol. 17 no. 3, (1986), pp. 1–14; CMEC (1986) *op. cit.*, p. 20 and Wuester, *op. cit.*, pp. 154–158.

[19]Anne Marie Decore and Raj S. Pannu, 'Educational Financing in Canada 1970–71 to 1984–85: Who Calls the Tune, Who Pays the Piper?' *The Canadian Journal of Higher Education*, vol. XVI no. 2 (1986), pp. 27–49 and Bruce W. Wilkinson, 'Elementary and Secondary Education Policy in Canada: A Survey,' *Canadian Public Policy*, vol. XII no. 4 (1986), pp. 535–572 which also contains an excellent bibliography on a comprehensive range of educational issues.

[20]Pat Hutcheon review of Philip H. Coombs, *The World Crisis in Education: The View from the Eighties* (1985) in *Canadian Journal of Education*, vol. 11 no. 2 (1986), p. 203 also reviewed by Sir Roger Bannister in *Interchange*, vol. 17 no. 3 (1986), p. 65 where he points out a number of salient financial questions raised by Coombs indicating that we do not have sufficient knowledge of finances, their effect and various organizational alternatives.

[21]David K. Foot, 'Youth Employment in Canada: A Misplaced Priority?' and F. Vaillancourt and Irene Henriques, 'The Returns to University Schooling in Canada,' *Canadian Public Policy*, vol. XII no. 3 (1986), pp. 499–506 and 449–458 respectively.

[22]The balance sheet boondoggle is discussed nicely in: 'Ottawa Issues Report Card on

Support of Postsecondary Education,' *University Affairs*, vol. 27 no. 4 (April 1986), p. 5. See also: W.R. Duke, 'How Should Education Be Financed in the 1980s?' *CEA Convention Proceedings* (Vancouver: CEA, 1980), pp. 6–17.

[23]Several comprehensive works not mentioned elsewhere are included in the bibliography. See: Edward Sheffield *et al.*, (1982); Hugh A. Stevenson and J. Donald Wilson (eds.), (1977); J. Donald Wilson (ed.), (1981); Wilfred B.W. Martin and Allan J. Macdonell (eds.), (1978); and Leonard Stewin and Stewart McCann (1987) and Ratna Ghosh and D. Ray (eds), (1987).

[24]B.W. Wilkinson, *op. cit.*, pp. 552–553 outlines the elementary-secondary situation with reference to recent work appearing in the *Canadian Journal of Economics* by Martin Dooley and that of Claud E. Forget in the *C.D. Howe Institute Commentary* (Montreal: The Institute, 1986). See also: reference note 28; Wuester, *op. cit.*, pp. 154–158; J.W. George Ivany and Michael E. Manley-Casimir (eds.), *Federal-Provincial Relations: Education Canada* (Toronto, OISE Press, 1981); Council of Ministers of Education, Canada, *Changing Economic Circumstances: The Challenge for Postsecondary Education and Manpower Training* (Toronto: CMEC, 1985), p. 15 and elsewhere and *Postsecondary Education Issues in the 1980s* (Toronto: CMEC, 1983) which contains some of the most intelligent commentary on the subject. See also: Dennis J. Dibski, 'A Federal-Provincial Partnership is Needed in Education,' *Education Canada*, vol. 21 no. 1 (1981), pp. 36–41 and John Grant, 'The Educational Role of the Federal Government,' in Winchester (1984), *op. cit.*, pp. 25–40; Dennis Dibski, 'Why Not An Office of Education for Canada?' *CSSE News*, vol. XI no. 6, (1984), p. 5.

[25]Allan Sharp, 'President's Message,' *CAUT Bulletin*, vol. 34 no. 2 (February, 1987), p. 3.

[26]Teresa MacNeil, 'Challenges and Opportunities in Canadian Adult Education,' *Learning*, vol. IV no. 3 (1986), p. 9 published by The Canadian Association for Adult Education. See also: Continuing Education Review Project, *Project Report: For Adults Only* (Toronto: Ministry of Colleges and Universities, 1986) and Skill Development Leave Task Force, *Learning A Living in Canada* II vols. (Ottawa: Employment and Immigration Canada, 1983).

[27]One of the most articulate expressions of maintaining the status quo is: J. Holmes, 'Post-secondary Problem Solving,' *Policy Options*, vol. 3 no. 4 (1982), pp. 39–46. See also: Walter G. Hardwick, 'Who Should Control and Deliver Education?' *CEA Convention Proceedings* (Toronto: Canadian Education Association, 1980), pp. 1–5.

[28]Bill Rompkey, 'National Education Strategy Should Be Top Priority,' *University Affairs*, vol. 28, no. 1 (1987), p. 18. See also: John J. Bergen, 'The Councils of Ministers of Education in Canada and West Germany: How They Work — What They Do,' *Education Canada*, vol. 14 no. 3 (1974), pp. 20–28.

[29]'Signs of Commitment are Encouraging,' *University Affairs*, vol. 27 no. 9 (1986), p. 7; 'Liberals Set Policy on Postsecondary Education,' *Notes from AUCC*, no. 86–21 (1986) p. 1 and Donald C. Savage, 'Liberals Adopt Resolution on Creation of PSE Council,' *CAUT Bulletin*, vol. 34 no. 1 (1987), pp. 1 and 6.

[30]*Ibid.*, and Council of Ministers of Education, Canada, *Principles for Interaction: Federal-Provincial Relations and Postsecondary Education in Canada* (Toronto: CMEC, 1985), pp. 1–6.

[31]See: David Vice, 'Post-Secondary Education in Canada: A Capital Investment. An Address to the Senate Committee on Finance,' Mississauga, Ontario, 1986; 'The Education Crisis,' *Globe and Mail*, May 12, 1984; several articles in *University Affairs*, vol. 27 no. 10 (1986); James C. Rush, and F.T. Evers, *Making The Match: Canada's University Graduates and Corporate Employers* (Montreal: Corporate-Higher Education Forum, 1986) and David Vice, 'Bold Action, Strategy Needed,' *Western News*, January 22, 1987, p. 13.

[32]J.D. Wilson, R.M. Stamp and L-P Audet (eds.) *Canadian Education: A History* (Toronto: Prentice-Hall, 1970), Chapters 18–21.
[33]Douglas Myers (ed.), *The Failure of Educational Reform* (Toronto: McClelland and Stewart, 1973), p. 59.

Response

Harry K. Fisher

With considerable wit and wisdom, Hugh Stevenson has reminded us of the vastness and complexity of public education in that vast and complex land that we know as Canada. And he has pointed out quite correctly that we know very little about the dynamics of that enterprise we call public education — an enterprise that consumes large amounts of resources; that is conducted in many settings; that is made up of a number of complex sub-systems that tend to be polarized within themselves; that employs and involves a significant portion of our population; that continues to try to respond creatively in an increasingly complex society and that commands an acknowledgment that it is truly central in our lives.

We have had presented to us a clear reminder of the impact on public education of the forces of social, economic, cultural and political change. Public education is linked in a complex way to the processes of social and economic development and it has been shown to us again that public education has a heavy responsibility to continue to contribute to that development.

Stevenson has attempted to look at the questions and issues that face us in public education as those questions and issues have emerged in relation to the backdrop of the Canadian social, cultural and economic context. May I isolate a few points in the presentation for particular comment:

(a) Stevenson's paper presents a story that has been characterized and formed by significant waves of change. But these changes should not be exaggerated. Clearly the period since 1970 has seen massive spending to accommodate and open up education to large and diverse populations; the rise of teacher unionism and power; the development of intermediate bodies in higher education and the beginnings of the application of informative technologies to learning, curriculum design and pedagogy. The next period will bring its own changes but observing the current scene through my work and the involvement of my own children, I sometimes reflect that very little has changed. I would suggest that the main goals and hopes for education held for the past twenty years are just as valid today. As the intensity of the voices of business and industry occur at the moment, they reflect in their urgency the fundamental aspirations for education as being as central to the development of Canada as before.

(b) I would have liked to have had some comments about the heady, indeed euphoric developmental period of the '60s as a foundation for the period since the '70s. The period of Stevenson's analysis was dominated by a shifting demography, economic recession, high levels of unemployment, rapid technological change and marked shifts in social and political attitudes — all of which I fear have propelled him to a present sense of despair at various points in his presentation. The positivism, the optimism and the excitement that we could argue was present in the '60s provides a historical balance over the longer strategic term. It has been said elsewhere that a 50 to 60 year time-frame is probably the best construct within which educational policy can be judged.

(c) Stevenson has identified the increased questioning concerning public education that is one qualitative feature of our current position. That position has to be appreciative of several more recent elements that form the context of the new intense inquiry. He touched upon the variety of social groups and sections of the Canadian population clamoring for a place. A desire for greater access is attended by the demand for a greater say in the creation of educational policy. Women and our multicultural communities are but two current sectors demanding changes in public education that will reflect their interests.

The intensity of our interrogation and reflection and the forces of change bringing about politicization were described briefly by Professor Stevenson. Issues of power and conflict attend this politicization. Debate has become more complex and the role of educational policy makers has become very problematical. These same policy makers face a troubled economic and social environment where general consensus on anything has become very fragile indeed. Education, as we have had it described, has moved outwards into a new definitional space that is susceptible to the intense forces of groups, advocacy centres and special interest sectors.

(d) Stevenson has reminded us that our current concerns about the quality of education in Canada are not unique. It might be useful to enlarge upon this point for just a moment.

One can refer to the efforts of Canada's associates, for example, within the Organization for Economic Cooperation and Development (OECD). The recently released report, *Japanese Education Today*, by the United States Department of Education and the forthcoming companion study by Japan on American education mark comparative studies of some significance and interest to educators in Canada.[1] Further, the International Conference on Quality in Education held in Washington D.C. in 1984, sponsored jointly by the United States and the OECD, provides a useful set of key factors for us in Canada as we continue to create our policy responses to the quality issue.

I would like to cite a few of these factors and using elements spawned by Stevenson's paper make a few comments from a Canadian's perspective.

(i) National goals should be clarified, and redefined if necessary. This remains an exercise of some frustrating complexity in the case of Canada, yet I hold to the hope that in our time, the partners in the many-layered structure of educational governance in this country will achieve some consensus in stating the goals for education in Canada. This fundamental factor alone could go a long way towards establishing a much needed foundation upon which policies for quality could be built.

(ii) We should continue to aim to enable all students to acquire a set of basic learning skills through the adoption of a national foundation curriculum characterized by balance, breadth, relevance and appropriate differentiation.

This is one factor or target that I suspect the public can identify with, yet attempts in the past have failed. One suspects we have an implicit national foundation curriculum housed within the curriculum guidelines of provincial authorities responsible for education. And it is with no cynicism at all that one could speculate that a national foundation curriculum for Canada lies truly with the textbook publishing industry. But who knows? We might achieve this objective in the next 5 or 50 years.

(iii) We should try to ensure that there is a good match between teacher qualifications and teacher tasks, that there is within each school setting a range of skills to deal with all learner needs and abilities and that there is competent management and deployment of resources.

Public education in Canada in the last twenty years, as Stevenson has said, has evidenced considerable growth in meeting the needs of students at risk and students requiring special education. The education and re-education of teachers is currently under analysis in several provinces, many of the states in the United States and it will be the main theme of the International Conference on Education in 1989 in Geneva.

The Canadian Teachers' Federation, following the lead of the Ministers of Education in 1982–1983 is championing the notion of interprovincial portability of teacher certification. There are instances where significant emphasis is being given to exchange programs and international enrichment programs. The idea, however, that the education of teachers and other educational leaders, should be seen as human resource development targets of national concern in Canada, and that they should be addressed as a national concern, continues to go nowhere.

Stevenson said that 'Canada rather desperately needs to get its educational and political acts together before the nation is left behind in a fast-moving world where the laggards court epithets of irrelevance and public disdain.' A national target founded upon the development of educational leadership at all levels could be one sector of national activity in getting our educational and political acts together in the interests of quality.

(iv)   The OECD has pointed out that another key factor associated with the quality of education is the development of effective leadership through close collaboration among students, teachers, Principals, parents and members of the community.

Stevenson, on this point, has reflected upon the politicization of these partner groups over the past 15 years and the growing frustration of an increasingly aware public with the dug-in, politicized, self-serving and strident voices of key influential elements of the educational establishment in this country. Something will have to give. There will have to be a greater rationalization of power and our next few years are going to be marked by activities that will seek ways and means to induce a more positive collaboration by the stakeholders in the educational enterprise.

(v)   Fifthly, the quality dialogue inevitably calls for effective ways and means of assessing educational progress within schools and at community, regional and national levels. Repsonses to this factor are underway in Canada, province by province — British Columbia, Alberta, New Brunswick,

Quebec, and recently Ontario with a newly announced scheme for testing senior English.

It has always seemed paradoxically Canadian that Ontario and British Columbia can compare with a certain degree of confidence, their performance scores in junior high mathematics with similar scores in Norway and Turkey through the International Evaluation Association. Yet as a parent from Perth County, I have no ready access to, or awareness of, evaluation data of a comparative nature with neighbouring jurisdictions such as Waterloo County. Indeed, I would anticipate that logged evaluation data over time for beginning students as maintained by the universities might be my only source of the kind of evaluation measures that I as a parent might find comforting when considering the quality of education at the present time.

A few concluding points:

(1) All of us — policy makers, administrators, researchers, school leaders and teachers — are well aware that it is easy to set out the aims for quality strategies as we have found in the OECD reference but it is extremely difficult to implement them. Stevenson's historical analysis has pointed out some of the reasons behind this enormous difficulty, including the basic structure of Canada. In addition, and this should be stressed, we know far too little at this point about the definition and interaction of factors of change that might help us to achieve success. Some very useful research has been accomplished but we could use a greater program of systematic and long-term research into the dynamics of effective change in education at this critical junction in our educational policy determination.

(2) The scope of both of the papers this morning is vast, yet I would have welcomed a more particular discussion about post-secondary education and its institutions as they contemplate their position within public education in Canada. Sessions III and IV on our program, however, will undoubtedly deal with issues that are rooted in higher education.

(3) Note has been made of several of the insightful, persuasive and respected public voices that continue to remind all Canadians of the state of higher education and the implications for our economic and social futures. Within the community itself, and many similarly insightful, persuasive and respected voices are here today, much has been accomplished in bringing our political and educational policy determinants to the critical apex that I agree is at hand.

This session has been devoted to historical and contemporary critical assessments. Clearly the area of higher education, and perhaps more than any of the other sectors of education as described by Stevenson, will have to guard its mission while responding creatively to the pressures of long-term unemployment and the melding of training and adult education and recurrent education; the nurturing of the humanities and the arts as key variables in coping with our social understanding of technological change, to cite but two conditions of policies for quality found on the contemporary scene.

Stevenson has lauded the role since 1970 of many educators who have demonstrated a sense of enlightened criticism of public education — voices which have alerted us to our point of current concern. While I would agree that this has been a responsible and very professional behaviour, I am not convinced that the voices have been seen, except by other educators, as having been of significance. We might speculate that education lacks voices of criticism in all sectors that serve on a continuing basis to educate the populace and stimulate concern and/or fear in the hearts and minds of educational politicians.

I do hope Professor Stevenson is correct in his analysis when he expresses a hope that public education is in a state of re-awakening to three policy dimensions:

— a firm faith in the value of public education;
— a belief that we can achieve funamental reforms to meet rapidly changing circumstances; and
— a recognition of the national dimensions to our concerns.

I am encouraged that this uniquely designed program by AUCC has been created for us in 1987 in Hamilton. It cannot but help with the re-awakening to these policy dimensions.

Notes

[1] United States Department of Education, *Japanese Education To-day* (Washington, D.C.: U.S. Government Printing Office, 1984).

3   Teacher Education in Faculties of Education: An Assessment and Strategies for Achieving Excellence

Naomi Hersom

Province by province, over a period of about two decades, the Canadian public education system has turned to the universities to prepare virtually all teachers for certification. Prior to 1960, the universities were expected to assume major responsibility for preparing teachers largely for the secondary schools. This required, so it was believed, little more than a sound education in one, or perhaps two of the arts or sciences required for the school curriculum, and the briefest possible introduction to life in classrooms with a nod in the direction of pedagogy. The normal schools or teachers colleges were responsible for producing the much larger supply of teachers, mainly women, who were needed to staff the elementary schools. Principals and school system administrators were usually drawn from the ranks of the men in the secondary schools, expected to learn by doing, typically by being placed first in the unfamiliar setting of an elementary school and then moving 'up' to become Principals of secondary schools or to become School Superintendents or Inspectors.

The overall effects of these earlier arrangements can be found in the teacher education programs in our universities today. Programs for students aspiring to become secondary school teachers continue to place major emphasis on subject area specializations and to give relatively little attention to pedagogy. Gender is still strongly associated with grade levels, with the choice of teaching specializations and with access to administrative positions.[1] Faculty members in the university at large tend to think in terms of programs focusing on the disciplines. Faculty members in education departments are stretched between the demand to demonstrate excellence in the practice of professional skills on the one hand, and the demand to meet academic requirements associated with research and scholarly activity on the other. Providing suitable laboratory experiences in classrooms continues to be problematic for the universities and for the school systems in terms of time commitments and additional, substantial costs.

With the influences of the past weighing so heavily on present practice it is rather remarkable that teacher education programs in Canadian universities have achieved any significant change during the last two decades or so. Before going on to assess the current status, I will review briefly the two main types of programs currently being offered in Canadian universities in terms of their general characteristics, and then I will comment on some possible alternatives based on the body of comparatively recent research and study being devoted to the field of teaching and teacher education.[2] The effects of strategies for improving teacher education programs on the quality of something as complex as Canadian public education are difficult to ascribe but I am assuming that good teachers and good administrators are fundamental to the achievement of excellence in education.

Characteristics of Current Teacher Education Programs

The existence of two main types of teacher education programs in universities across Canada is largely a matter of provincial history and tradition. They have been shaped, perhaps more than most university programs, by the combined forces of political coalitions, the growth of professional associations, economic change, university funding formulas, the demands of parents, employers and special interest groups, and the influence of practices elsewhere. They have seldom been based primarily on the results of research or careful policy analysis. There is very little evidence recorded that defines the advantages of one type of program over another. The arguments about the advantages or disadvantages of each type have frequently revolved around such factors as institutional cost-benefits, the art of the possible, and the formation of coalitions among interest groups. More recently, there seems to have been a growing awareness that the study of curriculum and instruction and the study of the historical, philosophical and social perspectives on schools and schooling are important considerations. This in turn has led to a recognition that these studies should be accorded greater emphasis in teacher education programs.[3]

Teacher education programs in Canadian universities fall into two broad categories. *Consecutive* teacher education programs require the completion of an undergraduate degree before applicants are admitted to a separate program leading to certification. *Concurrent* teacher education programs combine studies in the liberal arts with laboratory experiences in schools and classes in curriculum and instruction throughout the duration of the program. In the latter case, all requirements must be met before a student can be recommended for a degree and for certification. Each program is characterized by the ways it accounts for three major concerns in teacher education: Who should be admitted and how should applicants be selected? What should intending teachers learn in order to qualify for professional practice? What kind of classroom performance must be demonstrated before initial certification is granted? Experience has shown that the kinds of knowledge, skills and attitudes associated with the standards for the teaching profession and the expectations of the university are also significant factors to be taken into account.

Who shall teach?

Generally speaking, selection and admission procedures for applicants to teacher education programs have not extended very far beyond the usual requirements for admission to a general degree program in most Canadian universities. Whether the applicant applies at the first year level or after completing one or more degrees, standards across Canada for admission and selection seem to be related primarily to demonstrated adequacy in terms of the records of academic achievement that the applicant brings. This state of affairs is partly a legacy of those periods when the supply of teachers for the nation's schools has been stretched beyond its limits, a phenomenon that occurs cyclically. It is probably influenced as well by the reality of the difficulties encountered when universities and teachers representing professional interests try to identify reliable predictors of good teaching performance. However, there is some evidence that the candidate's record of academic performance, the professional assessment of the candidate's potential for skill development, and the candidate's expressed attitudes towards teaching are three criteria having some validity for prediction of success.

Using these criteria as general guidelines one can compare the relative strengths of the consecutive and concurrent types of teacher education programs in terms of selection and admission. The applicant to a consecutive type of teacher education program holding an approved degree has a proven record of academic achievement at the university level. The applicant to a concurrent type of program, entering university for the first time or after one or two years in a general program, is unproven beyond whatever level of reliability is to be found in the grades used as predictors of success. In both types of programs admission interviews are often conducted by individuals or teams within the university, and in some cases by panels that include representatives of the profession and of the general public as well. The selection of applicants following such interviews has tended to lean heavily on the informed judgments of the faculty and others who have been involved. Limited research has been conducted on the use of interview instruments and their validity as predictors of skill in teaching, although recent studies at the University of Saskatchewan show promise of some possibilities for further developments along these lines.[4] Other universities have been experimenting with the use of panels of interviewers and most programs depend on close cooperation with teachers and administrators in schools for screening candidates at some stage.[5]

Those programs that incorporate practical experiences in classrooms at a very early stage provide opportunities for students themselves to assess their own commitment and compatibility to teaching as a career. Such an arrangement also provides opportunities for faculty members and teacher supervisors to observe students in action in school settings and serve as another means for screening applicants before recommending for certification. Perhaps the most extensive and well-developed use of this approach to selection is to be found in the programs at Simon Fraser University although all universities incorporate faculty recommendations and professional consultation to some extent. A distinct advantage to the concurrent type of program lies in the several possibilities provided over time for the university, the student and the profession to be selective in terms of potential for successful practice.

In the case of teacher education programs following the completion of an approved degree, selection may be affected more significantly by the student's decision to apply after having completed more extensive academic studies and perhaps, after having assessed employment opportunities in alternative fields as well. Although a later rather than an earlier choice point may indicate a stronger commitment to teaching as a career on the part of the applicant, there are two other factors to be weighed whenever consecutive sequencing is used. There is a danger that delayed initiation to the classroom results in a higher withdrawal rate which is costly in terms of the sense of failure for the student who becomes a dropout at that stage and for the university and the schools in terms of their investment in the placement and supervision of such students. Allied to this factor is the lack of time available in the program for students to develop adequate teaching skills, to become familiar with classroom practice and to learn the specific content of the school curriculum. Not only is it necessary to have sufficient time to develop professional skills and knowledge in actual practice but also it is necessary to have time to reflect on that practice.[6] On balance it seems fair to say that the concurrent types of programs offering a graduated series of practicum experiences including an extended practicum of at least one full term in length and followed by a year of internship as an induction to the profession have relatively greater potential for excellence in professional preparation.[7]

What knowledge is of most worth?

Debates about curricula for teacher education programs frequently focus on the question of a proper balance between learning what to teach and learning how to teach. Consecutive programs requiring a completed undergraduate degree for admission place a good deal of weight on the importance of gaining an adequate general education along with some specialized knowledge in one or two subjects associated with the school curriculum before attempting to introduce students to the study of professional knowledge and practice. In many such programs the professional studies component has been assigned a period of one academic year or a little longer. To date, only a few of the consecutive programs that require studies in curriculum and instruction and in the historical, philosophical and psychological foundations of education amount to two additional academic years beyond the first degree.

Curricula for concurrent programs generally reflect a greater balance between the relative weights assigned to the liberal education components and to the professional education components required for the degree. In such programs, the sequence of courses and practicum experiences is specifically designed to allow time for the student to develop the knowledge and skills required for successful entry to the teaching profession. Accordingly, students are introduced to professional components in parallel sequence with studies in the liberal arts and areas of specialization on the assumption that the student will benefit by having opportunities to bring the understandings gained through the study of the disciplines to bear more directly on matters of professional practice.

Although there is a dearth of information based on research done in Canada that might throw light on the question of the relative amounts of emphasis to place on the acquisition of general knowledge and on the development of professional insights and skills in the curricula for teacher education programs, there is some indication that the graduates of the two types of programs perform differently in classrooms at the outset of their careers.[8] Students who have opportunities to study and practise the sciences of education over longer periods of time are more likely to be viewed by teacher colleagues and administrators as competent, based largely on perceived ability to plan and organize work in the classroom in ways that are appropriate to the grade level and to the type of students being taught. On the other hand, some critics of the curriculum content selected for teacher education programs view this as a drawback. Such critics claim that by socializing students successfully, graduates are unable to create change in the schools. However, those studies that have been carried out in actual classroom settings provide rather compelling evidence that beginning teachers should not be expected to override the forces of social and organizational expectations represented by the schools and the communities they serve.

Further, the results of such research suggest that professional skills should be well developed by students before full responsibility is thrust upon them. High attrition rates are costly in terms of personal losses for the students, in terms of investment losses for the universities who prepare them and in terms of the losses such early withdrawals represent to the future development of the teaching profession, to say nothing about the effect on the supply of teachers needed for the nation's schools. It seems only reasonable to recognize the importance of the role of professional studies in the curriculum for teacher education and to get on with the task of doing the research and development required to identify the content and nature of such curricula. It is surely unacceptable to dismiss studies in education using a clever turn of phrase made famous by the Canadian historian who titled her book *So Little for the Mind*.[9] That time is past. The findings of the studies now being done on teaching and teacher education and growing recognition on the part of the scholarly community for its responsibility for the quality of those who will be teachers are indicators of serious and long overdue interest in improving and strengthening teacher education curricula.[10]

Can the art of teaching be taught?

All teacher education programs require that students demonstrate ability to teach acceptably under supervision in schools or in other formal educational settings in order to become eligible for certification. The proportions of time allotted for laboratory experience and practice in classrooms varies greatly from province to province and among universities. The degree of involvement on the part of faculty members, practising teachers and administrators also varies widely. In fact, questions about the optimum length of time and the nature of practice have been the focus for most of the research that has been done on teacher education in Canada.[11] But the level of demonstrated competence deemed acceptable and the means of evaluating that level of competence in order to decide whether or not a student ought to be recommended for certification are issues that continue to be highly problematic.

Concurrent programs are designed to introduce students very early on in their university studies to the realities of life in classrooms, the presupposition being that students should have ample opportunity to assess their own commitment to pursuing a career in education. Experience has demonstrated that the initial assignments to school and classroom responsibilities are a watershed point for some. Consistent with a model of professional development over time, students in concurrent programs ideally are required to complete a graduated series of observation and practice experiences assuming greater and greater responsibility for teaching and managing the classroom. When this ideal is most nearly achieved, there is likely to be greater probability for successful entry to professional roles and for retention in the teaching force.[12]

To provide a varied and graduated series of experiences that are carefully structured and well-supervised by faculty members and by members of the teaching profession is a costly factor in pre-service programs. It requires commitment of faculty time and sufficient administrative support to organize school placements, travel, and arrangements for accommodating students and faculty off campus. Most importantly,the development of professional supervisory skills by faculty and cooperating teachers constitutes an additional demand on resources. Provisions for the study and practice of clinical supervision together with an expectation that faculty members and their colleagues in the schools who are responsible for the practice will undertake such preparation have not generally been accorded high priority by the universities despite the centrality of the practice to the quality of teaching.[13]

Fortunately there has developed a body of knowledge growing out of the study of teaching which is being used to inform professional practice. There is also a growing amount of evidence that clinical supervision can be used effectively to develop and strengthen the practice of good teaching and classroom organizational skills.[14] The uses of various types of performance analysis, including the rigorous use of videotaped lesson presentations, has greatly assisted students and teachers in learning how to improve the effectiveness of their teaching. It is reasonable today to claim more confidently than we have been able to claim in the past, that the basic skills undergirding the art of teaching can be deliberately taught and fostered throughout the whole of a teacher's professional career.[15]

Issues of Quality in Teacher Education

When Canadian universities undertook responsibility for pre-service teacher education they also assumed a larger role in a highly complex web of relationships that encompasses several levels of government, several different departments within government, teacher organizations, special interest groups, school trustees, parents, employers, and taxpayers in general who have concerns about the quality of public education. While interested people within the university may wish to devote themselves primarily to matters of curricular concern and research, people outside expect the university to pay attention to such issues as the supply and demand of teachers, provisions for continuing professional education, regulations governing the issuance of certificates, and ways to accommodate the growing demands for specialists capable of teaching students who differ widely in age, ability and background. It is beyond the scope of this brief assessment to address the whole range of issues affecting the perceived quality of the university programs in education. Rather, I will attempt some assessment of the general areas of strength and weakness in Canadian teacher education as perceived from the point of view of a former Dean of Education now turned university President concerned with the quality of those who graduate from teacher education programs in Canada.

Areas of Relative Strength

Universities in my view have enhanced the quality of teacher education in Canada in at least four major ways. By extending the requirements for a liberal education as a basis for professional study and practice in programs for students aspiring to be teachers in elementary schools as well as for those intending to teach in secondary schools, the universities have ensured that a significantly greater proportion of the population, (primarily made up of women and minority group members) have completed an undergraduate degree than might have been the case if elementary teacher education programs had remained outside of the universities.[16] Also, better educated teachers in elementary schools bring broader understanding to the task of preparing curriculum content and more informed understanding of the human sciences to guide their instructional plans.

By supporting research in teaching and teacher education the universities have contributed to the formation of a growing cadre of researchers who are systematically studying the factors that contribute to quality teacher education. The findings of their studies are beginning to influence some provincial policy decisions as well as some of the changes being introduced within universities designed to enhance the academic and professional strengths of their graduates.[17] By reconstructing the design and sequence of practicum experiences and by increasing the proportion of time devoted to them, the universities have assured greater possibility of success in initial teaching assignments and a higher probability of retention in the profession for its graduates.[18] In addition, the knowledge generated through research and professional practice in schools has contributed significantly to the development of career-long professional development programs and has facilitated efforts to implement changes in teaching methods or curriculum content.[19] By opening programs in ways that prepare teachers to serve all children as effectively as possible, the universities have increased accessibility to educational opportunities for all Canadians.[20]

Areas of Perceived Weakness

Because teacher education is of vital concern to parents and their children, to trustees and the publics they represent, to the teaching profession, as well as to the universities, it is often criticized on widely different grounds. Parents and students want and should have the services of excellent classroom practitioners, school boards and governments want teachers able to instill in the young the skills and attitudes appropriate to future citizens, the profession wants graduates who will bring vitality and creativity to its ranks, and the universities look for scholars and researchers. Each of the major areas of perceived weakness in teacher education to some degree respresents one or more of these several points of view.

In addition, there is a tendency in Canada to be overly influenced by arguments put forward by those expressing concern about the conditions affecting teacher education in the United States. The widespread publicity accorded the recent reports sponsored by prestigious American groups have focused public attention on the plight of teacher education in that country.[21] Although there may be somewhat similar sets of concerns in Canada, caution should be exercised about assuming that the same conditions obtain in our provinces.

Thus major areas of weakness in teacher education have been variously attributed to the level of academic achievement of those who apply for entry, to the level of general and specialized knowledge possessed by graduates, and to the level of skill in management of the classroom and in organizing the curriculum that is demonstrated in practice. Professors in Faculties of Education in Canada have been criticized for lack of a strong research tradition and schools are criticized because the application of research findings has been regrettably slow.[22] The matter of accessibility to teacher education for members of minority groups is problematic when the longstanding traditions of university entrance requirements are challenged by the realities of Canadian plurality and demographic change. Surrounding all of these issues are the cyclical conditions of teacher supply and demand and changing expectations for the role of schools and for the curriculum, which taken together create new and different bases for criticizing teacher education.

Strategies for Achieving Excellence

While some strategies for achieving excellence in teacher education are primarily dependent on provincial government policies and school system practices for their success, there are a number of strategies that can be initiated by the universities and implemented with the cooperation of other interest groups. Deliberate recruitment may not be necessary during periods when there are more than enough applicants to fill all of the places available in Canadian teacher education programs, but selection procedures should always be in place. These can be improved by using criteria associated with future professional credibility as well as with past academic performance. Interview protocols and other measures that are reliable and valid have been developed and are now available for use in Faculties of Education.[23] Requiring more years of study and greater amounts of practicum experience in order to qualify for teacher certification are strategies that have potential for gains in the acquisition of background knowledge and in the level of performance in the practice of professional skills. But it is important that extended time for preparation be structured carefully to ensure that additional academic and professional studies and field experiences will contribute to the development of strong candidates for the teaching profession. The universities in cooperation with the schools and the teaching profession can participate actively in the process of inducting teachers into the profession by providing appropriate seminars, workshops or other support services during an internship year.[24] Universities can give formal recognition to supervision of interns as an academic function appropriate to members of a professional faculty.

Perhaps one of the most important strategies for achieving excellence in teacher education is to instill the expectation that professional growth and learning constitute a career-long endeavour. To that end, Faculties of Education can plan appropriate sequences for continuing professional education programs and for graduate programs. Rather than perpetuating the traditional notions of the omnicapable teacher for elementary schools and the subject specialist for secondary schools, new programs can be developed for teachers who will become experts in alternative modes of teaching; for example, through the use of distance education techniques, writing computer programs, performing before the television camera, and conferencing with students through computer and telephone networks. The concept of creating programs in support of a master teacher rank which can be suitably recognized has potential for ensuring greater retention of good teachers in classrooms.

Universities can support partnerships with school systems in order to facilitate an exchange of information about the realities facing teachers in classrooms and information about new knowledge being developed by scholars and by researchers. Faculty members in various disciplines can be encouraged to address problems related to public education in their research and to work in collaboration with faculty members in education. Universities can take the lead in acknowledging publicly the importance of good schooling to the future of each individual and ultimately to the future economic and social well being of Canada. Although such endorsation may seem somewhat self-serving because the future for university scholarship and research also depends on the quality of the graduates from high school who choose to enter our universities, it is important for the university to underscore the long-term potential of the investments made in preparing excellent teachers for primary and secondary schools.

The University Milieu for Teacher Education

Faculties of Education were founded in Canadian universities, at least in part, on the belief that universities are best equipped to foster the proper development of a cadre of well-educated women and men who will be the teachers of the future. When the normal schools were amalgamated with the universities it was argued that opportunities for more advanced study and research would be the foundation on which to build a strong profession whose expert practitioners would improve the quality of teaching in the schools and thereby contribute to the overall quality of Canadian public education. It is timely now for universities to assess the extent to which we have fulfilled our mandate and to determine a vision of what our mandate should be in future. It is certainly timely for universities to re-affirm publicly the importance of good teachers and good schooling in Canada and to examine the leadership roles we should assume in achieving excellence in teacher education.

It is not sufficient, however, for the universities to focus attention only on such matters as the standards of academic achievement required of applicants or the appropriate balance between academic and professional studies in teacher education. Quality of practice in the long run is central, and it springs from something greater than intellectual aptitude or early demonstration of teaching skill. Such quality requires an investment on the part of the communities in which teachers serve, on the part of the governments that fund schools and universities and on the part of those who are members of the teaching profession. The universities are, I believe, poised in a position well-suited to provide the leadership needed to bring these forces together, to develop strategies for improvement in teacher education and to work together for their implementation.

This leadership requires something beyond the knowledge that good universities traditionally do provide to students based on scholarship and research. It requires that the universities recognize the importance of the task of preparing those who will become the exemplars of educational purpose and of societal values, teachers who must find ways to arrange disordered arrays of symbols and bits of information into meanings that can be understood by their students in turn and will serve to illumine the life-long thinking of those students.

Beyond the political leadership we in the universities can provide in aggregating the public will to support excellence in teacher education today there lies the historic realm of university leadership that aspires to creating a society characterized by the highest qualities of the human mind and spirit. We can strengthen the role of that historic leadership in teacher education as well. Although it may not be accorded the same attention it once was given, such leadership remains vital to the quality of all university programs, and especially to those offered in the professional faculties such as education. The question of how to address the issues in practical terms in our day is difficult to resolve.

In a recent essay, Green offers a way of approaching this aspect of the university's responsibility for leadership in teacher education by taking seriously the importance of 'the formation of conscience.'[25] Programs in Faculties of Education that encompass opportunities for students to learn how to judge their own conduct, each in their own case, will achieve an excellence that lies beyond scholarship and the canons of well-informed technically competent teaching. Further, Green suggests five aspects of his concept of conscience as criteria for excellence. The first is the extent to which teacher education addresses the development of a sense of craft: the capacity to experience satisfaction in something well done or to experience shame at slovenly work. The second criterion is the way teacher education instills the recognition that teachers must act for the sake of others in ways that do not cause others needless pain, something Green describes as the conscience of membership. The third criterion of excellence is associated with demonstrated ability to judge when to override the pursuit of self-interest in order to perform acts that extend beyond the limits of ordinary duty. The fourth is to be found in the ways that the memory of the long heritage of educational experience is used to inform professional judgements. And lastly, there is the criterion of respect for the imagination of poets and prophets, respect for those who question the presuppositions and pretensions of our day, respect for ideas that urge faculty and students alike to explore new realms of possibility.

The achievement of excellence in teacher education cannot be attained by universities acting unilaterally. Excellent people will be attracted to teaching when they know they will benefit from having a rigorous intensive initial preparation program and when they know that the schools will expect them to exercise responsible judgement as their part in the collective responsibility for schooling in our society. Teaching is an ancient and honourable profession. Canadian universities can provide a milieu for teacher education that contributes a sense of meaning for the graduates which will permeate the school curriculum they will teach and the manner in which they teach it. For it is the sense of meaning which excellent teachers give to their teaching that is the ultimate touchstone to quality in teacher education.

Notes

[1] See, for example, F. Echols, 'Applicants' Characteristics Relate to Performance,' *Teacher Education News* (UBC), no. 3 (June–Dec, 1986), pp. 7–8.

[2] Peter Grimmett and his colleagues at the Centre for the Study of Teaching, University of British Columbia, have been instrumental in bringing together Canadian scholars interested in theory, research and practice in teaching and teacher education. See Grimmett, *Research in Teacher Education: Current Problems and Future Prospects in Canada* (Vancouver: U.B.C., 1984).

[3] For example, two recent reports prepared respectively by the Ontario Association of Deans of Education(1982) and by the Deans of Education at Alberta Universities (1984) contain recommendations that more time in teacher education programs be given to the study of educational foundations, curriculum and pedagogy.

[4] H. Savage discussed this in a paper on the structured interview as a selection technique in which he described the results of using the Teacher-Perceiver Instrument in the process of selecting candidates for teacher education programs at the University of Saskatchewan. See 'Interviewing as a Selection Technique,' paper given at the annual meeting of the Canadian Society for the Study of Higher Education, Montreal, May 1985.

[5]In British Columbia, Simon Fraser University has depended on teacher associates for this purpose; at one time the University of Victoria assigned teachers who were on secondment from the school systems to serve on interview panels to screen applicants; and at UBC formal selection committees were established to select applicants for the five-year Special Education program.

[6]Ryan in an article published in *Teacher Education News* (1986) provides a brief description of the way Schon's work on 'reflection in action' is influencing teacher educators in Canada.

[7]This argument is made convincingly by the Deans of Education in Alberta universities in their report entitled *The Education of Teachers in Alberta: A Model for the Future* (1984) incorporating a six-stage plan for career development.

[8]A survey of principals by Unrah indicated school administrator preference for hiring graduates of programs that emphasize well-supervised, sequential practicum experiences. See W. Unrah, *Evaluation of the Faculty of Education* (Calgary: University of Calgary, 1981).

[9]Hilda Neatby, *So Little For the Mind* (Toronto: Clarke Irwin, 1953).

[10]For example, the National Commission for Excellence in Teacher Education report, *A Call for Change in Teacher Education* was published in 1985, a report by the Holmes Group *Tomorrow's Teachers* was published in 1986 as was the report by the Carnegie Forum on Education and the Economy, *A Nation Prepared: Teachers for the Twenty First Century*.

[11]See M. Wideen and P. Holborn, 'Research in Canadian Teacher Education,' *Canadian Journal of Education*, vol. 11 (1986), pp. 557–83.

[12]This issue has been addressed by J. Lyons and W. Stephan in a paper presented at the Western Association of Sociology and Anthropology Conference in Brandon (1983) reporting their study of students preparing to become high school teachers at the University of Saskatchewan.

[13]Wideen and Holborn, pp. 564–567.

[14]P. Grimmett, 'Clinical Supervision and Teacher Thought Processes,' *Canadian Journal of Education*, vol. 6 (1981), pp. 23–29.

[15]B.R. Joyce and B. Showers, 'The Coaching of Teaching,' *Educational Leadership*, vol. 40 (1982), pp. 4–16.

[16]See Statistics Canada, *Universities: Enrolments and Degrees 1972–73 to 1985–86*; *Fall Enrolment in Universities and Colleges*; and *Degrees, Diplomas, Certificates Awarded by Degree Granting Institutions*, for information prior to 1971–72.

[17]The use made of an evaluation study by Ratsoy, Babcock and Caldwell at the University of Alberta is one example of such influence. See E.W. Ratsoy, G.R. Babcock and J.C. Caldwell, *Evaluation of the Education Practicum Program, 1977–1978* (Edmonton: University of Alberta, 1978).

[18]The Faculty of Education at the University of Regina working in cooperation with the Saskatchewan Teachers' Federation has published materials such as *Learning to Teach — A School Responsibility*, a manual to assist interns, cooperating teachers and faculty advisers (1981) and *Internship Seminars for Interns and Supervising Teachers*, a book for participants (1981–82) in support of their programs.

[19]M. Fullan, *The Meaning of Educational Change* (Toronto: Ontario Institute for Studies in Education, 1982).

[20]For example, Native Indian teacher education programs are offered by several universities, frequently in off-campus locations, to accommodate the special needs of people living in remote and sparsely populated areas of Canada.

[21]National Commission for Excellence in Teacher Education, *A Call for Change in Teacher Education* (Washington: American Association of Colleges of Teacher Education, 1985).

[22]L. McLean, *et al.*, (eds.), *Research on Teaching in Canada* (Toronto: Ontario Institute for Studies in Education, 1982).

[23]Savage, *op. cit.*, and C. Mamchur, 'Predicting Teacher Effectiveness: An Interim Report on a Proper Linear Regression Approach to Selection for Teacher Education in British Columbia,' *Teacher Education*, vol. 25 (1984), pp. 68–79.

[24]Holmes Group, *Tomorrow's Teachers* (East Lansing: The Holmes Group Inc., 1986).

[25]T. Green, *The Formation of Conscience in an Age of Technology* (Syracuse: Syracuse University Press, 1984).

Response

Valérien Harvey

Review of Characteristics and Assessment of Quality

Naomi Hersom's review of the past and current issues of teacher education since its transfer to the universities is rightly focused. One only wonders if the author has not practiced the art of excellence much before the expression became *à la mode*, since the situation she portrays might at times leave some of us in want of such accomplishments. A case in point is the observation that the concurrent type of program has indeed achieved some status on a university-wide scale.

My own experience leads me to believe that truly 'integrated' programs of quality have been accomplished mostly within Faculties of Education and especially those influenced by the professional orientation originating in the Normal Schools. Strongly resisted in the Faculty of Education and in the whole university, the integrated programs appear to have been realized for the training of primary teachers who continue to be perceived as members of a low status profession for whom a program based more on the professional aspects and on practice than on 'scientific' dimensions is acceptable.

But, for the more aspiring roles of teachers of the secondary schools and the colleges, do the 'pedagogical' and other 'professional' aspects deserve the name 'consecutive model'? Is it not 'icing on the cake' that is widely in favour, when such programs could be taken 'on the go', partially on top of one's 'scientific' load, whenever possible?

Why is the popularity of the 'concurrent' or 'integrated' programs not higher for the preparation of all teachers? Well, is it not as it should be? In the primary, one teaches, at the other levels, the students learn.

One feature of Hersom's paper is its emphasis on the 'art of teaching'. In fact, no formal mention is made of the 'science of teaching' or of pedagogy as a discipline. This, in itself, characterizes the development of teacher education over the last twenty years. At first the programs were guided by the idea (or the pretension) that at the university the programs should have a strong 'scientific' base, one that would help teaching attain the longed-for status of a full profession rather than a mere craft.

As Hersom correctly points out, the strong professional orientation fostered in Normal Schools not only endured but also was strengthened with the emphasis on the practical aspects of teaching and a closer connection with the schools. Some institutions, like the University of Sherbrooke, were strongest in that professional orientation in part because that institution had other strong professional orientations in other faculties (medicine, law, engineering, adminstration, etc.) and put a heavy emphasis on close supervision of practical training through its 'cooperative plan' and other heavily weighted practicum experiences.

With the development of research in education, typically fostered by the university standards of the Professor–Researcher and the availability of resources, the 'scientific orientation' in the programs was greatly enhanced but made its way mainly in the rapidly developing graduate programs. Little of it influenced to a serious degree the undergraduate programs specifically designed for teacher training. As Hersom points out, 'the programs have seldom been based primarily on the results of research or careful policy analysis' and she adds that 'there is little evidence recorded that defines the advantages of one type of program over the others'. Then, why should an eminent authority, no doubt scientifically oriented such as our presenter, favor one type over the others? I venture one hypothesis. Formal research results are not the only source of evidence that can stimulate action in the university as elsewhere. Her own experience and sensitivity to feedback from former students, expert teachers, administrators and other sources of information all point in the same direction: the programs having the characteristics she described are those that appear to be most satisfying to the various publics concerned. That is correct! They may also be highly related to quality performance and excellence. Perhaps that could eventually be demonstrated. Recognizing the value of programs based on strong 'professional orientations' is not debasing for the university. It probably should have come sooner for the best benefit of teacher education.

Rejection, however, of models and their ideological bases is not a one way street. The practising teachers whose values are closer to the practical, the technical, and the artistic dimensions of the teaching function have also been slow in recognizing the value of the scientific orientation, the potential of existing research, further studies that need to be done and to which they too could contribute. They could have influenced the recognition, now making its way, that more than one type of research exists. Perhaps scientific research can only be approached indirectly by the practitioners? While research training is typically for would-be formal researchers, teachers could profit from a training (however centered on the teaching tasks) in and by research in order to become 'consumers' of research. Also, producing research is not altogether out of reach for the practising teacher, provided that proper types of research designs are made available. Artisans and artists too are said to do research! But the kind of research that they do is invariably closely linked to their process of production.

Neither this process nor the diffusion of results follows the 'scientific' pattern. Practitioners in education can do research like that of the engineer which instantly results in a 'technological transfer'. Such a perspective opens up a new era for teacher education programs. It could help bridge the widening gap between 'professional' and 'scientific' programs.

Perhaps as dangerous as the pitfalls of the first phase of university teacher training is the tendency to search for *the* best program. We have to remember that merely proving an effective approach does not disprove the potentiality of other models. Provided that lessons learned from the 'integrated' programs are taken into account, the programs more inspired by the scientific/theoretical approach (as opposed to the professional/ technical and artistic model) could prove to be equally useful.

A pluralistic approach should be in order in our complex world and such an orientation should continue to foster the idea that differentially based programs ('scientific' and 'professional') should be in competition even for the undergraduates. There are indications that interest is growing for the scientifically oriented programs, provided that they are as pertinent and satisfying as their counterparts, which is the major challenge to designers of those programs.

The consequences of opening the range of programs rather than closing on the 'best' are numerous. Enrichment by diversification could challenge the process implied in the three dimensional task so ably demonstrated by Hersom:

(a) Who should be admitted?
(b) What should be learned?
(c) What initial performance should be demonstrated?

It would appear that while a common set of answers could be identified, typically around the organizational pre-requisites of classroom learning (if that technology persists), differentiated answers for the three questions could match the 'different but equal' orientations couched in programs based on ideologically and technologically divergent programs. Such diversity should be fostered by universities for the preparation and upgrading of practitioners of the art(s) and of and the science(s) of teaching.

Strategies and Invariants

Hersom's contention that our programs are lacking in 'social perspectives on schools and schooling' is, no doubt, an implied strategy for excellence, and one that I would like to insist upon. Research on the economic, social, organizational and political aspects of education lack so much that it leaves the school systems an easy prey to the 'research' done and widely diffused by the media.

Social research in education does not have to be well internalized by teachers to be useful to the system and it could help the practitioner cope with his or her practice situation. A major handicap, however, for this type of research to make its way to the teachers is intrinsic to its results. The results of research on social determinants of education consistently show how strong the environmental variables are, consequently how little the relative contribution of educators can be in the circumstances.

Thus, the teachers are constantly confronted with the difficulty of *valorization* in their work activity because of the heavy social invariants and daily working conditions. On the other hand, teachers are the favourite scapegoats, not only for educational declines, but also for the lack of competitiveness in the overall market. Such a heavy burden is perhaps alleviated by their participation in programs that are based on the professional ideology that the teacher indeed 'makes a difference'. This motivating factor may also be one reason for the success of the professionally oriented programs.

However, the burn-out producing effects of pressure to perform at least collectively despite the scarcity of resources and the teacher's incapacity to achieve the results expected is but one aspect of the less-than-excellent conditions in which teachers are expected to achieve excellence. Furthermore, there is an overwhelming social condition that is pressed on professional educators which comes from the public's belief in the all-powerful value of education in our society.

While it is important to contribute to the *valorization* of the profession by developing the qualities mentioned by Hersom in her strategies, we should also be aware that pressing for a sense of craft and sense of meaning can also add to the social burden put on teachers in the name of the value of education. I do not negate the importance of the sense of meaning and dedication, but I think we have to be careful not to give too much credit to what could be a return to a consideration of teachers as the new saints who should work for the worth of the cause, guided by abnegation and asceticism. Reforms in education are fostered by social recognition, decent pay and adequate working conditions. Teachers cannot be the saviours from the mistakes of a society that is taking risks with its investments in people.

Teachers seem destined to follow the path of the declining industries. Is it only a matter of time, however, before they are raised again on the 'altar' that really counts in our society — the social and economic one. Perhaps in the meantime it is well to remind them that teaching has always been a craft or a profession in which the best rewards were psychic: those having to do with the relationship with students and the intrinsic conviction that they do 'make a difference' even if it does not show and they are not recognized for it. Stressing generosity, however, to the point of sacrifice can be counter-productive.

Quality performance and excellence cannot be demanded from the educational sector any more than it can be fostered in other parts of society. Quality education does not depend on the educational system alone; teachers are only one part of the larger social system on which quality ultimately depends. Universities must make increased efforts in teacher education but they must also insist that other conditions be met in society so that the contributions of educators can be maximized.

Thus, an important dimension of quality in teaching resides in the social organization of the work of teachers. Why should we take the actual work organization of schools for granted when offices and even the manufacturing workplace are being changed? New technologies are being introduced that not only have to do with computers but also with the way we arrange the social relationships between humans and machines and the way in which we manage people.

What about the schools? What is foreseeable for that work organization? Will the media and the workplace take over? Since the direction that the educational organization will follow is important for determining the best strategies for teacher preparation we should start thinking about the trends that are likely to challenge the present system.

Of course educational systems change slowly and we are at least fortunate to have reasonable time to think through the complex variables that influence the quality of teaching in our schools. In these respects Naomi Hersom's analysis has given us a realistic place to begin making the improvements that many of us would undoubtedly like to see achieved.

Canadian Educational Research: An Assessment and Strategies for Achieving Excellence

Daniel R. Birch and David F. Robitaille

Our task is to examine the entire body of educational research in Canada, to pronounce on the state of its health and, having completed our diagnosis, to formulate a prescription for improvement. In taking on this prodigious assignment we feel a bit like country doctors who know their patients moderately well but, called upon to characterize a patient's general condition, become acutely aware that they lack the particular expertise of colleagues from dozens of respected specialties. Furthermore their bag of tricks does not include the nuclear magnetic resonance imaging or positron emission tomography available in the tertiary referral hospital. The press of caring for patients has encroached on their time for reading professional journals. What then can our country doctors bring to the task? They bring a concern for the patient and for the patient in the context of family and community and, fortunately, in this case they also bring access to a body of reports from specialists in a variety of disciplines and fields of study.

The State of the Art

Seven years ago the health of Canadian research in education received a thorough examination. At that time several sources of concern converged to bring about unprecedented participation in that examination. The President of the Social Sciences and Humanities Research Council (SSHRC), André Fortier, in speaking to the Canadian Association of Deans of Education (CADE) at Thunder Bay in March, 1981 declared;

> ... the Council does not see itself as merely a passive recipient of applications. Our responsibility as a dispenser of public funds demands much more. It demands a commitment to help ensure that subjects of universal concern attract the best research brains in the country, that perceived gaps in research are acted on, and that the

results of this research are made known widely and effectively across the land.

This we would like to do for research in education[1].

We will not review the antecedents of that commitment by SSHRC but rather concentrate on its consequences.

With SSHRC support three reports appeared in 1981 and 1982: *Canadian Research in Education: A State of the Art Review*, edited by John H.M. Andrews and W. Todd Rogers; *Education Research in Canada: Aims, Problems and Possibilities* by John J. Stapleton, Michel Allard, Donald A. MacIver, Eric D. MacPherson, and Thomas R. Williams and *Research on Postsecondary Education in Canada* by Edward Sheffield. These reports were sponsored by CSSE, CADE and CSSHE respectively.[2] Since this paper is concerned with research on elementary and secondary education, we will not consider further the CSSHE report. A fourth report was undertaken in-house for SSHRC and appeared in 1982: *Education Research: Future Expectations and Past Performance* by Miles Wisenthal.

In coordinating the CSSE study, Andrews and Rogers identified ten areas of specialization and selected one or more outstanding scholars to undertake a state-of-the-art review of each field. Those scholars in turn put together teams, requested submissions or obtained interview data from colleagues in their own and related fields. The ten designated 'areas of specialization' were educational psychology, educational foundations, early childhood education, special education, adult education, counselling, administration, curriculum and instruction, measurement and evaluation, and teacher education.

Rogers and McLean estimate that 'about 110 people were closely involved in the total project.'[3] Consequently the SSHRC/CSSE state-of-the-art review constituted a massive self-assessment by Canadian educational researchers. To return to our analogy, it also represented diagnoses by ten teams of specialists. You will recognize, however, that each 'field' in itself represents a wide range of sub-specialties, whether disciplines, particular client groups or fields of professional practice.

The CSSE study culminated in a list of 24 wide-ranging recommendations,[4] many of which have since been adopted and implemented by SSHRC. Andrews and Rogers recommended,

> that education be identified by SSHRC as a high priority area for furthering the national interests of Canada and that SSHRC feel free to employ funding policies which do not limit the amount or kind of research in education because of provincial sensitivities.

These first two recommendations are important for several reasons. Firstly, the historical division of constitutional powers in Canada makes education a matter of provincial jurisdiction. The federal government, however, retains overriding powers in matters of national interest, the basis for federal support in higher education. The authors were suggesting that *research* in education also be defined as 'in the national interest' thereby justifying federal participation in a field that might otherwise be seen as falling exclusively under provincial jurisdiction.

Secondly, SSHRC includes in its interpretation of its mandate a commitment to;

(a) Support such discipline-based research as in the judgment of scholars will best advance knowledge;

(b) Encourage research on subjects which the Council, in consultation with the academic community, considers to be *of national importance*;

(c) Facilitate communication among scholars in Canada and abroad, and stimulate the dissemination of research;

(d) Assist in, and advise on, maintaining and developing the national capacity for research.[5]

Beginning in 1979 SSHRC had established several strategic thematic grants programs in areas considered to be of national importance. Andrews and Rogers anticipated the possibility of education becoming the focus of such a strategic grants program.

Thirdly, it had been widely perceived that research closely related to educational practice had been and would be considered by the Council as a matter of provincial or local jurisdiction and, therefore, ineligible for SSHRC support. Such perceptions were, at least partially, grounded in direct experience.

... no less than 23% of all education proposals submitted to the SSHRC from 1975 to 1980 were considered ineligible, transferred or withdrawn. The vast majority were considered ineligible because they proposed the preparation of materials designed to measure curriculum effectiveness, a purpose considered to be beyond the purview of Council and a matter of provincial concern.[6]

Wisenthal notes that more than 90 per cent of the applications deemed ineligible were 'in the curriculum and pedagogy specialities'. On the basis of his review of proposals from 1975 to 1980, he provides examples of proposals ruled ineligible for what he judged to be 'inadequate reasons', e.g. studies of sex education and moral education, of mathematics instruction, and of text books in relation to national identity.[7]

Fourthly, the CADE report showed that, in 1980/81, of the $12.5 million total awarded to scholars in Faculties of Education in the form of grants and contracts for research, development and evaluation, less than six per cent had come from SSHRC. Although much of the scholarly activity was directed to the solution of specific problems in policy and practice, findings of such studies are frequently relevant beyond the immediate institution or local jurisdiction in which they are based. The total amount, $12.5 million, is certainly not a large investment in Research and Development for education, a $20 billion enterprise. The SSHRC contribution, however, was less than half a million dollars. Thus the national contribution was too small to have any significant influence on the direction or quality of Canadian research in education. To provide a reference point, we note that a 1983 internal SSHRC report stated that Canadian federal support for self-initiated, non-contractual research in education was ninety times smaller than American.[8]

Andrews and Rogers emphasized the importance of supporting 'high quality research at all points on the theory-practice dimension'. In so doing they were responding to a SSHRC practice of emphasizing research related to the development and elaboration of theory. The CSSE recommendations endorsed as important 'generalizable studies involving curriculum development and evaluation, . . . Canadian replication of research done elsewhere, . . . the replication and extension of work done in a particular province or region,' and 'policy research . . . expected to have generalizable applicability'.

Five of the recommendations dealt with broadening the range of research activities in education considered appropriate for SSHRC funding and two further recommendations with reorganization within SSHRC in order to handle proposals more effectively. Fundamental to these was the creation of a separate adjudication committee for education, together with appropriate allocations of research funding and Council staff. Members of the adjudication committee and assessors were to be drawn from the ranks of prominent, Canadian educational researchers. Two recommendations addressed the need to identify through a broadly based consultative process 'priority areas for research of national interest which would serve as the focus for programmatic research'.

SSHRC moved rapidly to declare research in education a priority, to revise procedures and to establish a separate adjudication committee to consider research proposals in the field. Extensive participation in the state-of-the-art review of Canadian research in education, generally rising expectations for faculty research productivity, regional and national discussion of the research agenda in various sub-fields, the emergence of research institutes and the fostering of improved research proposals all contributed to a sharp increase in the number of grants awarded and the total funds awarded for research in education.

The data in Table 1 show that the number of SSHRC-funded projects in education increased each year from 1981/82 when the Education Committee was set up through 1985/86. A decrease in 1987 coincided with a change to a single annual competition. If major grants are excluded, the average annual amount awarded for any given proposal remained more or less constant over a five-year period with a reduction in 1987.

Table 1 *Social Sciences and Humanities Research Council Research Grants in Education° Allocation by Year, 1981–1987 (In thousands of dollars)*

Year	Regular Grants			Major Grants		
	Grants	Project Years	$	Grants	Project Years	$
1981/82	15	18	487			
1982/83	28	34	778			
1983/84	29	40	958	1	3	718°°
1984/85	42	71	2,447			
1985/86	68	96	2,470	1	3	479°°°
1987 Spring	59	86	1,850			
TOTAL	241	345	8,990	2	6	1,197

°   Grants awarded through the 'Education' Committee. A few education grants are awarded to scholars in other fields (e.g. Psychology, Family Studies and Child Care) and Professors of education obtain grants through other discipline committees of SSHRC (e.g. History, Psychology and Sociology), as well as through the Natural Sciences and Engineering Research Council (NSERC). Grants in the latter two categories are not included in this report.

°°   To OISE (Michael Connelly), Alberta (Heidi Kass) and Memorial (Robert Crocker)for the Second International Science Study. Crocker was on SSHRC at the time and his share of the project's funding was provided by Memorial University rather than by Council.

°°° To SFU (Philip Winne, Wolfgang Rothen and Ronald Marx) for 'Models of Teacher and Student Cognition for Artificially Intelligent Software.'

Beyond the significant increase in funding for research in education through its 'discipline-based research grants', SSHRC confirmed 'Education and Work in a Changing Society' as a priority theme for strategic grants with an annual allocation of $500,000 beginning in 1986/87. In the preceding year SSHRC funded regional workshops for the development of research proposals and more than 100 researchers participated.

Between 1979/80 and 1986/87 SSHRC established six themes for strategic grants designed to encourage research on subjects considered to be of national importance. In the order of their adoption the themes are Population Aging, Managing the Organization in Canada, Family and the Socialization of Children, Human Context of Science and Technology, Women and Work and, finally, Education and Work in a Changing Society. Strategic theme programs are expected to encourage both disciplinary and interdisciplinary research and education scholars have been successful in obtaining support under all six themes. (see Table 2.) Managing the Organization is the theme under which the state-of-the-art review was funded but, apart from that venture, it has been little used by education scholars, a somewhat surprising fact in the light of large graduate enrolments in educational administration.

Table 2 Social Sciences and Humanities Research Council Strategic Theme Grants to Scholars in Education (In thousands of dollars)

Year	Population Aging P.Y.°	$	Managing the Organization P.Y.	$	Family and Socialization P.Y.	$	Human Context of Science P.Y.	$	Women and Work P.Y.	$	Education and Work P.Y.	$	P.Y.	Annual Total $
1979/80	1	10											1	10
1980/81	4	96	2	50									6	146
1981/82	3	33	1	8	2	65	3	11					9	117
1982/83	4	63			5	179							9	242
1983/84	2	33			5	221	3	15	9	50			19	319
1984/85					7	107	4	84	2	70			13	261
1985/86	2	30	1	5	6	167	5	121	5	55			19	378
1986/87	4	122			12	516	3	17	7	220	9	169	35	1,044°°
TOTAL	20	387	4	63	37	1,255	18	248	23	395	9	169	111	2,517

° Project Years
°° Includes funding awarded earlier but applicable in 1987/88 and beyond

Canadian Faculties of Education

We have said little thus far about the milieu of Canadian educational research. The establishment of education as a field within Canadian universities on any substantial scale has taken place entirely since World War II. With one exception, a primary mission of education units in universities has been, and continues to be, the pre-service education of teachers. In most cases, former normal school faculty members, selected for excellence in both teaching and in teaching teachers, constituted an influential subset of the faculty. Others were recruited in their image. Most faculty members shared responsibility for supervising student teachers, often for extended periods and at great distances from the university.

Throughout the sixties and most of the seventies, Faculties of Education were swamped by the challenge of bringing the teaching force up to the level of a first degree and increasing teacher–education enrolments to meet the demands of growing school systems. At the same time large numbers of teachers, librarians, counsellors, administrators and would-be administrators swelled the size of magistral programs and were encouraged to do so by the structure of negotiated salary scales. Those faculty members qualified to teach at the graduate level were assigned evening and summer courses, and often given unrealistically large numbers of graduate students to supervise.

This characterization of Faculties of Education may sound like a rationalization to justify a minimal output of scholarly work. In fact, many scholars in education demonstrated extraordinary commitment to research and maintained remarkable productivity under the most challenging conditions. But, even in the early 80s, these productive scholars were not the majority of the 3,000 plus faculty members in education.

Nor has funded research activity been distributed proportionately among institutions. Of $12.5 million awarded in 1980/81 to scholars in Faculties of Education in grants and contracts (for research, development and evaluation broadly defined), almost two-thirds went to three institutions: the Ontario Institute for Studies in Education, the University of Alberta and the University of British Columbia.[9] Analysis of the data presented in Table 3 shows that, although not quite as heavily concentrated, competitive research funding from SSHRC is skewed. Two institutions (UBC and OISE) received more than 30 per cent of the total funding (35 per cent of strategic grants). The next 30 per cent was awarded to five (Alberta, Montreal, UQAM, Simon Fraser and Memorial) while 11 institutions shared a further 25 per cent. Thus from 1980 through 1987, 85 per cent of the SSHRC funding for education research went to 18 faculties and institutes. The balance was spread among about two dozen institutions and one dozen private scholars.

Competitive research funding remains fairly concentrated with almost 90 per cent of SSHRC education research dollars going to scholars in 20

Table 3 Social Sciences and Humanities Research Council of Canada Support for Research in Education (Through Education and Strategic Theme Grants, 1979–1987) (In thousands of dollars)

Institutions Receiving $150,000	Education Regular Grants			Strategic Theme Grants			Education Major Grants			Total SSHRC Awards			Rank
	Grants	P.Y.	$	Grants	P.Y.	$	Grants	P.Y.	$	Grants	P.Y.	$	
British Columbia	37	52	1,528	18	23	490	1	3	359	55	75	2,018	1
OISE	23	37	1,207	10	13	387	1	3	359	34	53	1,953	2
Alberta	7	10	347	9	9	94				17	22	800	3
Montreal	17	28	667	3	4	130				20	32	797	4
UQAM	12	20	470	5	8	263				17	28	733	5
Simon Fraser	8	11	170				1	3	479	9	14	649	6
Memorial	11	16	502	5	5	36				16	21	538	7
Saskatchewan	6	9	391	1	1	15				7	10	406	8
Guelph	5	8	157	2	5	245				6	13	402	9
INRS	7	11	391							7	11	391	10
McGill	8	12	347							8	12	347	11
Laval	8	12	286	5	6	57				13	18	343	12
Sherbrooke	5	8	226	4	5	61				9	13	287	13
Queen's	6	8	254	1	1	5				7	9	259	14
Victoria	5	6	97	2	4	155				7	10	252	15
Laurentian	1	1	21	2	3	195				3	4	216	16
Concordia	6	6	139	2	2	33				8	8	172	17
Calgary	5	8	132	3	3	14				8	11	146	18
Sub-total	176	263	7,332	72	92	2,180	3	9	1,197	251	364	10,709	
Other Institutions (25)	50	63	1,127	16	17	218				66	80	1,361	
Private Scholars	15	19	531	2	2	119				17	21	650	
TOTAL AWARDS	241	345	8,990	90	111	2,517	3	9	1,197	334	465	12,704	

institutions. However, the patterns have shifted somewhat over the first six years of the program. Table 4 presents the dollar value of research grants for the 'top twenty' with the rank and percentage of total funds obtained by each. By dividing the period into two segments of three years, we can see some evident trends. In the first segment one institute (OISE) accounted for one-third of the total, three accounted for almost 60 per cent and only 14 received a substantial allocation at all. In the second segment the top institution (UBC), by more than doubling its research funding, retained its previous share at 15 per cent and no other institution obtained more than nine per cent. Sixty per cent of the funding was allocated to eight institutions rather than three, and 19 received a substantial amount.

Perhaps the most striking trend is the performance of Quebec universities which collectively increased their SSHRC funding for education research very substantially, not only in total dollars but even in percentage, moving from 19 per cent to more than 30 per cent of a much larger total. The province of Quebec maintains an internal program of rigorously competitive research funding as do some other regions. Most provinces also emphasize the value of obtaining an appropriate 'share' of funds from national programs.

The Growth of Research in Education

To say that research in education reflects is social milieu is to state the obvious. This is true in part because social concerns are frequently reflected in funding priorities, and researchers are not insensitive to such influences. The issues of burning interest to policymakers will inevitably be prominent in the consciousness of researchers. Furthermore, major complex social issues tend to be intrinsically interesting, perhaps particularly so when problems are challenging and even appear intractable.

Torsten Husen provides three examples of the influence national concerns have had on the orientation and type of educational research.[10] Firstly, in England following the 1944 Education Act which legislated provision of secondary education for all according to ability, a generation of research was directed to enhancing the efficiency with which eleven year olds could be sorted and sifted. Secondly, in Sweden during the same two decades educational researchers attended to the effects of selecting able students and educating them with or apart from the less able. How might a comprehensive educational system be devised to maximize the achievement of individual potential and equality of opportunity? Thirdly, in the United States in the sixties the issue of racial inequality was prominent and schools were expected to be a major instrument for achieving equality, for eliminating poverty and, in the post-sputnik era, for regaining lost American technical supremacy. Research and development in education received massive infusions of funds. Equality of educational opportunity was a

Table 4 Social Sciences and Humanities Research Council Regular and Major
Research Grants in Education° Allocation by Institution, 1981–1987 Top 20
Institutions

	1981–87			1981/82–1983/84			1984/85–1986/87		
	$	%	Rank	$	%	Rank	$	%	Rank
OISE	1,565	15.5	1	973	33.0	1	593	8.5	4
British Columbia	1,528	15.0	2	457	15.5	2	1,071	15.0	1
Alberta	706	7.0	3	359	12.0	3	347	5.0	7
Montreal	667	6.5	4	55	2.0	10	612	9.0	2
Simon Fraser	650	6.0	5	55	2.0	9	595	8.0	3
Memorial	502	5.0	6	207	7.0	4	295	4.0	9
UQAM	470	5.0	7	89	3.0	8	381	5.0	6
Saskatchewan	391	4.0	8	0	0.0	–	391	5.5	5
INRS	391	4.0	9	108	4.0	6	283	4.0	10
McGill	347	3.5	10	51	2.0	11	296	4.0	8
Laval	286	3.0	11	134	4.5	5	152	2.0	14
Queen's	254	2.5	12	40	1.0	12	214	3.0	11
Sherbrooke	226	2.0	13	31	1.0	13	195	3.0	12
Guelph	157	1.5	14	0			157	2.0	13
Concordia	139	1.5	15	0			139	2.0	15
Ottawa	135	1.5	16	0			135	2.0	16
Calgary	132	1.5	17	0			132	2.0	17
Trois Rivières	110	1.0	18	10			100	1.5	19
Lethbridge	106	1.0	19	0			106	1.5	18
Moncton	100	1.0	20	100		7	0		
Sub-total	8,873	88.0		2,669	91.0		6,194	87.0	
TOTAL	10,087			2,941			7,146		

° Includes all regular research grants awarded on the advice of the Education
Committee and two major grants, one in 1983/84 and one in 1985/86.

pervasive theme. The schools were to achieve it and Research and
Development Centres were to show the way.

What, then, are the particularly Canadian social issues detectable in
Canadian educational research? Not surprisingly, ethnicity, social mobility,
and multiculturalism represent themes growing in volume and diversity
throughout the past two decades — in both anglophone and francophone
literature. Language development, second language learning and bilingual-
ism are subjects of extensive research across the country. Wallace Lambert
and G.R. Tucker (McGill) and David Stern, Merrill Swain, P. Allen, *et al*
(OISE) are prominent among Canadian scholars with international reputa-
tions in these fields. Mary Ashworth, Bernard Mohan, Margaret Early,
Kenneth Reeder, Jon Shapiro, Rita Watson and Hillel Goelman (UBC)
work not only in ESL but in first language acquisition.[11]

The importance of multiculturalism in Canadian education was evident when Ronald Samuda, John Berry and Michel Laferrière obtained support from the Multiculturalism Directorate of the Secretary of State to assemble several dozen authors in a symposium from which emerged a text on the subject. Much research and development has been funded from that source — a prime example of an alternative to the granting councils. Jack Kehoe's research contributions culminated in his role as research director for the parliamentary committee which addressed issues of discrimination against members of visible minorities. Keith McLeod writes about policy and practice. Kogila Adam-Moodley brings to bear her sociological research on ethnicity in divided societies. Joti Bhatnagar adopts a comparative perspective and Vincent D'Oyley deals with issues of assessing ability and achievement in a context of cultural diversity.

It has often been said that Canada has too little history and too much geography. One of the by-products of a sparse population in a vast land is an emphasis on transportation and communications technology. Indeed, this was the dominant theme of EXPO '86. Distance education has developed in Canada with sophisticated satellite delivery of instruction. Research and development activities in this field — whether in Quebec's Concordia or British Columbia's Open Learning Agency — have led to major international projects in Asia and Latin America. These, in turn, have incorporated further research and development.

The first nations of Canada have, in the past decade, multiplied several times over their participation in Canada's universities and colleges. UBC has recently added a graduate program to its Native Indian Teacher Education Programme (NITEP) which now produces a steady stream of graduates. Two years ago the Mokakit Research Institute, a group of Native Indian researchers from across the country, was established. Under Verna Kirkness, its first President, attention to matters related particularly to aboriginal education led to a growing body of publications. A recent comprehensive examination of many aspects of Indian education is *Indian Education in Canada*, 2 vols. (Vancouver, 1986, 1987) edited by Jean Barman, Yvonne Hébert and Don McCaskill.

Chad Gaffield, a prominent Canadian social historian of the younger generation, made the following comments in the course of reviewing a book edited by J. Donald Wilson and David C. Jones:

> Since the late 1960s, the history of education has proven to be one of the richest fields of critical inquiry. In the context of new concern for theory and method, historians found a wide variety of subjects which had been ignored or inadequately addressed: school attendance patterns, educational ideology and literacy, to name only a few.[12]

Gaffield attributes to educational historians recognition of 'the importance of topics such as the history of ethnicity, labour, and women,' and states that it was they who 'breathed new life into a sometimes moribund discipline.' He accords them an eminent place in the emergence of Canadian social history and goes on to observe that the international impact of research on the educational history of Canada should not be underestimated.

Michael Katz of OISE, with his colleagues and students, pioneered fresh approaches to questions of literacy, schooling and education in nineteenth century Canada using census data and computer analyses. Neil Sutherland's work on the history of childhood, and the work of at least a dozen other education historians contributed to placing the history of education squarely in the centre of Canadian social history.

Emerging fields of interdisciplinary research not infrequently gain impetus from scholars in education. Roland Lorimer, in communication studies at SFU, continues to tackle issues of significance to education, e.g. his study of the process by which the 'Canadianization' of American school textbooks leaves the Canadian versions entirely void of any national symbols. Mary O'Brien and Alison Prentice of OISE are in the forefront of feminist research and have contributed much to the still emerging field of women's studies. 'Feminist education is the process by which our skills are utilized to bite the hands which have so confidently but parsimoniously fed us.'[13] Jane Gaskell's and Dorothy Smith's SSHRC-funded studies are contributing to our understanding of the sociology of work and the sociology of education with particular emphasis on the effects of social institutions on women.

Educational psychology is perhaps the most diverse and vigorous of fields in Canadian educational research.

> The quantity of Canadian research in educational psychology and its sub-fields is enormous. For instance, a brief survey of only two volumes (1979, 1980) of three major (international) journals (*British Journal of Educational Psychology, Contemporary Educational Psychology, Journal of Educational Psychology*) identified twenty articles published by Canadian researchers.[14]

Philip Winne, who commented thus on the vigour of his own field five years ago, today coordinates a team which has obtained a major SSHRC grant of almost half a million dollars over three years. Cognitive science and applied psychology are, indeed, particularly well represented at Simon Fraser and at OISE.

Some dimensions of educational research have particular relevance to Canada and serve to point out the importance of replicating in Canada, work done elsewhere. Barbara Holmes tested both British and American norms for five individually administered intelligence tests with a representative provincial sample. She discovered that British Columbian children, at the three age levels tested, scored significantly higher than those in the original normalizing samples. Thus, to use these intelligence tests appropriately, new norms were established for British Columbia. Other Canadian research such as that of Jaganath Das (Alberta) and Ronald Jarman (UBC) has contributed directly to the development of a new generation of intelligence tests in the United States.

Moral development, values education and critical thinking are central to our conceptions of education. Scholars from coast to coast emphasize research in these fields. Stephen Norris (Memorial) and Jerrold Coombs (UBC) both coordinate research programs in critical thinking. Clive Beck (OISE) and the Association for Values Education Research (UBC) are among many who address the role of the school in moral development and the implications for teaching. Their work extends from philosophical analysis to the development of curriculum materials, a span familiar to scholars in education.

With elementary and secondary education under provincial jurisdiction, with no federal office of education and with limited federal support for research in education, it is extraordinarily difficult to mount national research studies. Nevertheless the potential returns from doing so are very great and steps need to be taken to facilitate this sort of activity in the future. An alternative to a Canadian study, of course, is a national study in another country, the task Doug Willms (UBC) has carried out in the United States and again in Scotland. His expertise in quantitative sociological methods has gained him a prominent place in large studies of school achievement in relation to a variety of socioeconomic variables.

A prime example of a collaborative national project is the study of science teaching sponsored recently by the Science Council of Canada. The study, which was coordinated by Graham Orpwood and Jean-Pascal Souque, engaged teams of anglophone and francophone researchers from across the country in obtaining, analysing and interpreting a rich variety of data ranging from teaching materials and surveys of teachers, to classroom observations. The various sub-studies tell us a great deal about teaching and learning in Canada's science classrooms, including teachers' views of the nature of science and the way science is portrayed to students, the relationship between science and society, and teachers' priorities in science teaching.

Shortly before his death, George Tomkins completed a major history of curriculum in Canada, *A Common Countenance: Stability and Change in the Canadian Curriculum*. Although little about the study of curriculum has been uniquely Canadian, Canadian scholars have been prominent in the field. The first international journal of curriculum studies was founded in Canada as *Curriculum Theory Network* (now *Curriculum Inquiry*). Where once scholars regarded themselves as working in the field of science education or social studies education, today graduate programs, at least, tend to have a common core in curriculum studies staffed by educational philosophers, historians and sociologists as well as subject matter specialists. Michael Connelly has pioneered research on teachers' personal practical knowledge. Science educators like James Gaskell and Gaalen Erickson respectively are working with SSHRC funding to examine the social construction of the physics curriculum and to develop new paradigms in the Donald Schon tradition while exploring student's beliefs about scientific concepts. Patricia Vertinsky's research in physical education is historical and sociological in approach and LeRoi Daniels' work in law-related education draws on law and philosophy to address curriculum issues.

In its provision for nurturing the very young, a society reveals much of itself. Hillel Goelman and Alan Pence, with the cooperation of colleagues across the country, have undertaken several studies of the nature and quality of parental and professional childcare.[15] Their research is innovative and has the potential to contribute eventually to policy development. Such work, like the research in early language acquisition, although not set in schools, is relevant to public education. Early experience has implications for subsequent learning and the care of progressively younger children is, by public policy, becoming a shared responsibility of family and society.

Strategies for Achieving Excellence

Significant research in education is expensive — in human resources, in funds and in time, that much is abundantly clear. Public accountability for the use of public resources is important. How then can we increase the probability that scarce research funds will be used to good effect? We need to devise strategies to ensure that the research which is funded is of high quality and that it has the potential to contribute significantly to our understanding and, better yet, to make a substantial difference to policy or practice.

Not only must research in education be of high quality, it must also be focused. The field is so broad that the possibilities for avenues of research activity seem virtually without limit. On the other hand, funds are limited and we can ill afford to support non-programmatic research. Early in their careers, scholars need modest levels of support, much like that provided by NSERC. Subsequent awards should be based, in part, on the candidate's track record.

Accordingly, priority should be given to funding teams of researchers able to plan coherent programs of collaborative research. Such teams should be funded for several years with the expectation of continued support contingent on continued productivity. We should not hesitate to support strength even if it means concentrating resources. Karl W. Deutsch and his colleagues analysed 62 major advances in the social sciences from 1900 through to 1965. They found that most of the outstanding developments took place in a few major, urban centres; that an increasing proportion of advances were made by interdisciplinary teams of scholars; and that following initial breakthroughs, substantial research programs of ten to fifteen years followed. The concentration of social science achievements in particular centres was even more marked than the concentrations in modern physics and biology. They hypothesize that contributions to social science may be very sensitive to the presence of 'local sub-cultures with other first-rate investigators and facilities in other fields, as well as to an intellectual climate specifically favourable to social science.'[16]

Canadian scholars are frequently unfamiliar with the work of their colleagues across the country, particularly when that work has been published in the other official language. There may be good reason for francophone and anglophone scholars to undertake parallel studies, but not in mutual ignorance of each other's work. During her term as chair of the SSHRC Education Committee, Naomi Hersom lobbied diligently in support of a Canadian, bilingual database in education and this remains a strategic imperative. The Canadian Education Association (CEA) is working toward the development of such a database to supersede *Ontario Education Resources Information System* (ONTERIS), *Education Quebec* (EDUQ) and the *Canadian Education Index*.

International networking is important as well. Canadian membership in organizations such as the Stockholm-based International Association for the Evaluation of Educational Achievement (IEA), and nation-wide participation in projects sponsored by that organization need to be encouraged and facilitated. At the present time, individual provinces may participate, or a team of researchers may put together a national project, but the latter is a daunting task. Mariel Leclerc and Doris Ryan in the Classroom Environment Study; Michael Connelly, Heidi Kass and Robert Crocker in the Science Study; David Robitaille and Leslie McLean in the Mathematics Study are among the Canadian scholars who have given leadership in the international assessment of learning. Indeed, the Science Study was the focus of a major grant from SSHRC in 1983/84 (see Table 2.) We should investigate ways to have Canada participate in such activities at the national level, perhaps under the auspices of SSHRC as the funding agency, the Council of Ministers of Education, or a newly established inter-provincial consortium set up for the purpose of facilitating this type of cooperative activity.

Maintaining a research program at the forefront of one's field is the scholar's means of paying the dues required to maintain membership in the international 'club' of active researchers. Exchange of current work and participation in research symposia are among the benefits which flow from such associations. For example, although Sally Rogow is in a very strong department of Educational Psychology and Special Education, she is the only continuing scholar at UBC studying the education of blind children with multiple handicaps. Her extraordinary achievements ensure international recognition from which flows stimulating interaction with those scholars who invite her to serve as keynote speaker at a research symposium or external examiner at a foreign university.

Similarly research on teaching and/or teacher education of the quality of Robert Crocker at Memorial, Rodney Clifton at Manitoba, Al Mackay at Alberta, Ronald Marx and Philip Winne at Simon Fraser, Peter Grimmett or Marshall Arlin at UBC ensures constant interaction wth American research groups at Stanford, Texas, Michigan and Chicago among others. Both individual scholars and research groups depend on such constant contact and interaction for intellectual nourishment and greater, cumulative impact.

Each of the national granting councils (NSERC, MRC and SSHRC) is subjected to competing pressures from the major research institutions which would like to concentrate even further the limited resources available to support research and the institutions which lobby for programs designed to share the wealth, however limited it may be. We must be uncompromising in letting quality and performance determine the allocation (and perhaps, the concentration) of research funding.

Secondly, efforts should be made to enhance the quality of research supported through provincial funding. Scholars can be encouraged to embed important research studies in provincial learning assessment programs. David Robitaille and James Sherrill demonstrated the value of so doing when they contracted to undertake the B.C. Mathematics Assessment and published some of their findings beginning in the late '70s. Similar studies have followed in several other subjects and provinces. Moreover, agreements can be reached with provincial authorities to make the data banks resulting from learning assessments available to *bona fide* researchers, both faculty and graduate students. International studies coordinated through IEA provide extensive sources of data for additional analysis. Many valuable studies can be carried out without requiring fresh data collection for each.

The government of Ontario makes a grant of about $2,000,000 annually to OISE for research with the expectation that allocations will be made with provincial priorities in view. OISE manages a rigorous, peer review process using external assessors to help in the awarding of internal research grants. Were this practice followed in other provinces and territories, albeit on a smaller scale, both the Ministries of Education and the universities would be well served. Even greater coherence could be achieved were the Council of Ministers of Education, Canada to establish research priorities in areas of common interest and concern. This could be done with the help of a research advisory committee. The funding of parallel or complementary research studies in several provinces could enhance the power of the undertaking, especially with coordinated planning and execution.

Conclusion

Many of the recommendations for enhancing research in education suggest drawing more scholars into the enterprise. It is arguable that a better strategy would be to engage fewer investigators in research. Kjell Rubenson observes that there are too few departments where 'the knowledge is in the walls', where the ethos is overwhelmingly intellectual and there is some potential for research to be coherent, for findings to be cumulative. To follow his reasoning would lead to greater differentiation — both among institutions and among faculty assignments in a given institution.

Not only might faculty roles be differentiated but, conceivably, greater differentiation should be made between research-oriented graduate degrees and professional degrees. On the one hand greater emphasis could be placed on professional performance as an entry and exit criterion in the professional degree. Students seeking the research degree could be selected for high academic achievement in a discipline and substantial knowledge of the research tools and traditions of that discipline. Greater emphasis could be placed on providing a coherent, research-oriented program with progressive involvement in research activity — as a research assistant and subsequently, perhaps, as a co-investigator. From institutions and from fields characterized by these practices and reflecting a concomitant intellectual ethos outstanding scholars have come. Thus is a tradition of excellence in research established and built.

Ultimately it is the judgment of peers that determines the adequacy of research activity —both at the funding stage and in the review of outcomes. Marshall Arlin would apply the following judgment first to his own work, hence we grant him credibility when he claims that in our assessments we need to stress the criterion of significance . Unless a study has the potential to make a difference — to illuminate our understanding, to say something profound about practice — it cannot be characterized as excellent *educational* research. That is, technical quality and methodological rigour are necessary but not sufficient conditions for excellence. Statistical significance is not enough; educational significance must be our primary criterion.

Notes

[1] Andre Fortier, 'So Little for the Mind? Federal Support for Education Research.' Notes for an address to a meeting of the Canadian Association of Deans of Education, Thunder Bay, Ontario, March 4, 1981, p.11.

[2] The Canadian Society for the Study of Education (CSSE) and its counterpart in higher education (CSSHE) are the learned societies made up of scholars in those fields.

[3] W.T. Rogers and L.D. McLean, 'Promoting Educational Research in Canada,' *Educational Researcher*, vol. 16 no. 2 (1987), p.10.

[4] J.H.M. Andrews and W.T. Rogers (eds.), *Canadian Research in Education: A State of the Art Review* (Ottawa: Minister of Supply and Services Canada, 1982) pp. 12–31.

[5] Social Sciences and Humanities Research Council of Canada, *Annual Report 1984–85* (Ottawa: Minister of Supply and Services Canada, 1985), p.5.

[6] M. Wisenthal, *Education Research: Future Expectations and Past Performances* (Ottawa: Minister of Supply and Services Canada, 1982), p.5.

[7] *Ibid.*, p.9.

[8] Cited in Rogers and McLean, p.10.

[9]J.J. Stapleton, M. Allard, D.A. MacIver, E.D. MacPherson and T.R. Williams, *Education Research in Canada: Aims, Problems and Possibilities* (Ottawa: Minister of Supply and Services Canada, 1982), p.18.

[10]T. Husen, 'Educational Research in a Meritocratic Society'. Paper presented at the I E A General Assembly Meeting, Singapore, 1984, pp. 1–4.

[11]Names of education scholars are given as examples for a non-education audience. The authors apologize to the large number of able scholars who necessarily go unmentioned.

[12]Chad Gaffield, review of J. Donald Wilson and David. C. Jones (eds.), *Schooling and Society in Twentieth Century British Columbia* in *Labour/Le travail*, 8/9 (1981–82), pp. 401–2.

[13]I. Winchester, M. Holmes and H. Oliver (eds.), 'Illuminating Education: The Uses of Science, History and Philosophy in Educational Thought,' *Interchange*, vol. 17 no. 2 (1986), p.5. For a comprehensive anthology on the female experience as teachers and learners, see Jane Gaskell and Arlene McLaren (eds.), *Women and Education: A Canadian Perspective* (Calgary, 1987).

[14]P.H. Winne in Andrews and Rogers, p.178.

[15]Funding for these studies is included in Tables 2 and 3 above for consistency even though Child Care is not in Education at the University of Victoria and Guelph funding was in Family Studies.

[16]K.W. Deutsch, J. Platt and D. Senghaas, 'Conditions Favoring Major Advances in the Social Sciences,' *Science*, (February 1971), p. 458.

Response

Doris W. Ryan

Dan Birch provided a useful review of the current status of research in Canadian education and a thoughtful analysis of strategies for enhancing the quality and significance of educational research. In what follows, I will address my comments to two themes that run through the paper: (a) research in education reflects its social milieu and (b) significant research in education requires a differentiation among institutions and, within them, a differentiation among faculty roles.

Public schooling is one of the largest of our social enterprises. Since Faculties of Education have the primary responsibility for the pre-service preparation of teachers, they are themselves peculiarly public institutions with direct links with the external environment of the university. In many ways, the Faculty of Education must serve several masters: the general public, policy makers, the community of educational practitioners, and the academic community. These masters do not always share the same expectations or values for the roles of Professors of education. In general, the external public demand that significant resources be devoted to teaching functions and to what the university calls service functions. Educational research is accorded the most value by the external public if it is directly applicable to schools or to questions of educational policy and practice.

Geraldine Clifford argued recently that Schools of Education have disappointed themselves and others in their efforts to achieve applications of knowledge, and she traced this disappointment to the education faculty's allegiance to the academic community rather than to the teaching profession. Although Faculties of Education have tried to conform to the university's notion of the mission of a professional school, Clifford concluded that they have not convinced their academic colleagues that education is a defensible discipline; indeed, education schools have suffered 'chronic defensiveness' and 'congenital status deprivation.' Nevertheless, Clifford stated, education schools have consistently made the academic group their major public, 'no matter how unwelcome they are' in the academy.[1]

Dan Birch has commented on the recency of education as an academic field within the university. The emergence of graduate studies in education has been accompanied by increasing institutional pressures for faculty members to engage themselves in what, for many, is a new expectation: the conduct of scholarly research and the production of papers for refereed journals. Grapko's interviews with Deans and faculty members in a sample of Ontario Faculties of Education illustrated the pressures being felt, especially by newer faculty members seeking promotion and tenure. He noted that, while research projects need not be entirely 'incompatible' with services to school systems, education faculty members generally perceive that there will be a 'slow and gradual retrenchment from participation in the school system to do a detached study of the system, particularly for staff who can fit in with the research thrust.'[2]

The perceived 'pull-and-tug' of competing expectations is demoralizing for at least a portion of the faculty. In Fullan and Connelly's review of teacher education in Ontario, for example, the teacher educators with whom they spoke generally pointed out that many faculty members are untrained in doing research and that many have a heavy teaching load which does not allow time for research. Their interviewees noted, with disappointment, that there is little recognition in the universities for the services that Faculty of Education members provide to the teaching profession.[3]

In an insightful and provocative essay, Harry Judge observed that the trouble with graduate schools of education is that inevitably they have something to do with teachers, 'even if that something often means as little as possible,' and the trouble with teachers is that they are painfully undervalued.[4] Since the profession of teaching enjoys so little prestige, Judge argued, education cannot gain status within the university as a professional school and must turn to the arts and sciences school as a model. This dilemma is not one faced by other professional faculties, according to Judge, who wrote;

> The responsibilities of a Dean (of education) in so perpetually critical a situation are awesome. No wonder some Deans ... gaze wistfully across the water at schools of law and business. A law school is unabashedly in the business of training lawyers, and it does so with an easy confidence. Nearly all its faculty regard themselves as lawyers and practitioners, teaching is celebrated and rewarded, consultancy freely undertaken. There are few signs of dependence upon, still less of deference toward, 'outside' disciplines. The demand for places in the best schools and by the ablest students remains high.[5]

In short, the relative status of Faculties of Education and that of the profession they serve are interrelated. In my opinion, increasing the emphasis placed upon educational research has the potential to help improve the status of both groups. However, the university community must acknowledge that a major portion of educational research should be practice-oriented and problem-based. If we recognize that there is theory in all practice, educational research might well be both more significant in terms of yielding applicable knowledge and better understood and valued within the academic community.

How do we achieve excellence in educational research, given that 'excellence' may be defined somewhat differently by the academy, the teaching profession, and the general public? Birch has suggested that we need to concentrate limited research resources in centres of excellence, whether those centres be within particular institutions or organized to bring together colleagues from several institutions. Thus, he has called for a differentiation of roles within and between Faculties of Education. I agree wholeheartedly with Birch's strategy.

If we adopt a strategy of differentiation, it will be necessary to assess the potential for research participation within and among the Faculties of Education and to assess the additional resources needed to enhance the potential. It may be useful to compare some descriptive information about The Ontario Institute for Studies in Education (OISE), already a differentiated institution, with information about the ten Faculties of Education in Ontario.[6] For the academic year 1985–86, OISE had a full-time faculty of 138, some 88 per cent of whom held the doctorate. The Faculties of Education had from 15 to 89 faculty FTE's, and only from 33 to 65 per cent of these persons held the doctorate. OISE's 600 full-time and 1500 part-time students were all seeking graduate degrees. In contrast, the neighbouring Faculty of Education at the University of Toronto had 20 graduate students, 860 undergraduate students, and some 5100 students enrolled in in-service or Advanced Qualifications programs. While OISE had a total of 97 support staff FTE's for its faculty, the Faculties of Education had only from four to 60 support staff FTE's. Not surprisingly given its special mandate, around 70 per cent of the OISE faculty members were engaged in funded research,[7] but only from ten to 30 per cent of the faculty in the institutions included in Crapko's study reportedly had a funded research project.[8]

Much food for thought may also be provided by the experiences within OISE in providing support for research. During the past six years, we have moved to the kind of internal differentiation called for by Birch. We found that our nine departments were not providing adequate and stable support for those who wished to concentrate their work in research activities; in particular, few workload differentials were possible within the departmental structure. Thus, our Board of Governors approved a policy whereby research centres could be established to conduct work in important substantive or problem areas. The centres are organized under a senior administrator, and the time allocations (cross-appointments) of faculty members to centres are based upon the time reflected in their research proposals and grants.

University Presidents will appreciate that these structural changes have not been enthusiastically endorsed by the majority of faculty members who do not hold a cross-appointment to one of our five research centres. Nevertheless, the centre structure has allowed differential workloads and has made it possible for faculty members who wish to do so to devote a major portion of their time to research. The outcomes, in terms of visibility to funding agents and rates of proposal submission and grants, have been rewarding. For example, during 1981–82, the 22 faculty members in research centres were associated with research projects granted a total of $2.4 million; the 100 or so other faculty members (only 65 of whom were involved in funded research) had brought in $2 million. Analyses of the average workloads and research productivity of centre and department faculty members revealed that centre faculty did on average teach fewer courses (an average of two as compared with four for departmental colleagues), but they compensated for this by being engaged in many more research studies (an average of four per FTE as compared with one or fewer per FTE in departments) and reported far more publications for that year (an average of four per FTE as compared with 1.5 in departments). Moreover, the centre faculty had more thesis supervisions, especially at the doctoral level.[9] Internal differentiation may rub against the egalitarian grain, but it does appear to provide a fruitful means for meeting the critieria for excellence espoused by Birch.

In conclusion, I would encourage the presidents to give thought to their institution's vision for its Faculty of Education. I doubt that any of us would want those visions to be identical across institutions. The important point is to *have* a vision — an accepted and acceptable mandate for the Faculty of Education — which will have steering effects on resource allocations, on decisions about faculty hiring, and certainly on the priorities reflected in what faculty members do and how they spend their time.

Over the next several years, there will be opportunities to increase the research productivity of Faculties of Education through faculty hiring decisions and through decisions about workload differentials and supportive structural arrangements. The replacement of almost one-quarter of the full-time faculty members in Ontario's Faculties of Education, for example, will be possible because of retirements expected over the next several years.[10] Will they be replaced? Who will replace them? What will be the vision of the Faculty of Education during their tenure within the university community? If research in education is to be a priority for their work, and if that research is to be both scholarly and significant, there is much thinking and planning to be done. Birch's paper and the others presented in this conference provide a sound starting point for future planning.

Notes

[1] G. Clifford, 'The Professional School and Its Publics.' Unpublished address to a conference sponsored by the Benton Center for Curriculum and Instruction, The University of Chicago, May 15, 1987.

[2] M. Grapko, *The Role of Faculties of Education in the Implementation and Evaluation of Educational Change: Feasibility Study, Phase I* (Toronto: Ontario Ministry of Education, 1986), p. 10.

[3] M. Fullan and M. Connelly, *Teacher Education in Ontario: Current Practice and Options for the Future* (Toronto: Ontario Ministry of Education/Ministry of Colleges and Universities, 1987).

[4] H. Judge, *American Graduate Schools of Education: A View from Abroad* (New York: The Ford Foundation, 1982), p. 29.

[5] *Ibid.*, pp. 48–49.

[6] Data taken from Fullan and Connelly. *op. cit.*

[7] Data provided by the Office of the Assistant Director (Field Services and Research), The Ontario Institute for Studies in Education.

[8] Grapko, *op. cit.*

[9] Data provided by the Office of the Assistant Director (Field Services and Research), The Ontario Institute for Studies in Education.

[10] Fullan and Connelly, *op. cit.*

Response

J.W. George Ivany

The points regarding educational research already raised in the papers by Dan Birch and Doris Ryan are well worth elaborating upon. I shall expand upon two and add a third issue in the consideration of the quality of research in education. These are the following:

(a) The problem of jurisdiction, or the provincial–federal sensitivity for all matters concerning the discipline of education.

(b) The problem of associating and comparing inquiry in education with that in other disciplines, or what kinds of scholarship are legitimate, and necessary, in education?

(c) The need to consider the legitimate roles required in education and in professional faculties generally, or the failure to appropriately differentiate the professional from the scholarly requirements of faculty members in education.

Permit me to elaborate briefly upon each of these three. Federal–provincial disputes are not new to Canadians. The historical conclusion of the jurisdictional argument between the national and provincial governments in Canada about authority in educational matters may have been beneficial in some areas of concern. However, in the domain of research in education it has been a great hindrance. What other discipline suffers from such a dialogue? Can you imagine certain inquiries, seeking support in say, physics, in computing science, or even in that other provincial preserve — medicine, being denied funding from national granting councils because the particular question is seen by some as falling into provincial jurisdiction? Do you realize that the recent study of science in the public schools carried out by the Science Council of Canada[1] was impaired by the refusal of provinces to cooperate in the supply of relevant achievement data? The reason: this was a provincial matter, not of concern to, nor the business of, federal agencies. When we, at Simon Fraser University, conducted a conference on this topic of federal–provincial relations in education it was very strongly felt that the extent to which we could depend upon input from the members of the Council of Ministers of Education, Canada would depend upon our agenda and our list of presenters. Such an environment is hardly conducive to good research.

It was the opinion of the vast majority of participant scholars in the conference referred to above, which, incidentally, was held during the national dialogue on a new constitution, that some national presence was essential to education.[2] Whether this should be a new ministry, a department, a national office, was not clear. What was clear to all was that when the Federal Government spends hundreds of millions of dollars each year (out of more than 200 different programs and offices) in a uncoordinated, almost fugitive manner, national educational objectives are being poorly served. What is also clear is that when the Council of Ministers meets frequently and in camera, conducting itself as an unobserved and therefore unaccountable, national, educational body, Canadian education objectives are being poorly served.

One of the major losers in this contest for power is support for research into education. While education is one of the most pervasive and expensive of social programs, basic research into its operation remains poorly funded federally and funded almost not at all provincially.

The second theme I wish to elaborate upon concerns the nature of educational inquiry. The debate as to whether education is properly to be viewed as a discipline is pointless. That it is a field of human action of considerable complexity and deep interest is sufficient to predict its attraction as a focus of intellectual analysis. However, the debate itself does occur and is indicative of a misunderstanding about fields of inquiry generally. Not all scholarship follows the deductive, theory-driven models most completely demonstrated in the physical sciences. The attempt of social scientists in the past century to apply empirical methods is not inappropriate, but their attempt to claim for their disciplines the same kind of powerful models that exist in, say, physics can only be termed naive. Such claims have led critics to evaluate the theories against rigorous criteria and, inevitably, to find them wanting. Such claims have led critics to examine educational research, and that in other social sciences, and to be surprised that its knowledge claims are disjointed and non-cumulative. The problem is one of perspective.

The varieties of intellectual pursuit understood by the ancient Greeks are both the source of this problem and its solution. Joseph Schwab in revisiting Aristotle describes the 'Arts of Inquiry' as consisting of three types: the theoretic arts — which seek for ultimate truth; the productive arts — whose end results, whether artistic sculpture or engineering structures, are products of the intellect; and the practical arts — politics, the law, whose end results enable decision-making and action.[3]

Clearly, if physics or natural philosophy is the example *par excellence* of the evolution of this ancient, theoretic pursuit of truth, so education can be viewed as ultimately the pursuit of decision-making, of effective practice. Seen this way, the varieties of educational inquiry to be expected, to be desired, indeed, to be considered essential, wander widely from the controlled experiment. The problem for the university, and for research granting agencies, becomes finding the means to value and nurture such a varying and rich field of inquiry whilst still maintaining high intellectual standards. There should, then, be no debate as to whether creative and novel curriculum materials, for example, are appropriate artefacts of scholarship. Rather we should exhaust energy upon how to evaluate such products. Are they indeed unique? Are they sound translations of theory into practical application? Do they exemplify new pedagogical ideas? Surely these questions, and others, can be posed with rigour, and can be answered with confidence. And surely such questions are equally applicable under appropriate transformation to other pragmatic fields — engineering, business and medicine.

A more complicated issue for research in education, not unrelated to the previous discussion of the nature of the field, has to do with role differentiation in Faculties of Education. It is on this issue that I find myself most at variance with many of my colleagues. The misunderstanding that stems from this issue is not restricted to outsiders but is firmly entrenched within the education community itself.

Given the nature of the demands upon a Faculty of Education it is essential that a wide range of competencies and role models be resident in the faculty. This is not an uncommon problem. Universities have long differentiated the roles and responsibilities of Professors, lecturers, sessional instructors, teaching assistants, laboratory instructors, etc. The problem within Faculties of Education is the rarity of the concession that some vitally important skills and activities in teacher education are not intellectual or scholarly in any but the most trivial sense, — valuable, even essential, but not scholarly. Put another way, no teacher education program can have credibility without staff who, themselves, are master teachers, who have years of successful *and current* experience in real classrooms, who are expected to spend countless hours in the schools supervising students. Whether or not these individuals produce new knowledge, conduct research, write for scholarly journals, they are essential. But think of the nature of this scholar practitioner. By definition this is not a typical graduate as found in other disciplines. The requirement of years of demonstrated excellence precludes that. Even if this individual has acquired a graduate degree it will not be a degree pattern familiar to other disciplines. No bright young honours graduate this, but rather an experienced practitioner first and foremost, no matter what the earlier qualification earned. This new Ph.D., then, graduates side by side with the more typical scholar (more typical, that is, to other fields). He or she is hired side by side with the researcher as though they were meant to perform the same function, and as though they were equally prepared to succeed in the traditional tenure and promotion process. The obverse also exists in that graduate programs in education typically deny entry to bright young scholars from the cognate social sciences unless and until they have completed an education program and have taught in schools. I do not deny the utility of this practice, I merely exhume it here to illustrate that these graduates, who would be optimally prepared to win the tenure sweepstakes, are frequently excluded from the faculty, denied the opportunity to work as pure researchers applying their disciplines to problems of pedagogy.

This, then is the dilemma. The Faculty of Education, like others, hires doctoral graduates into tenurable, professorial positions. Graduate programs in education make little distinction among the needs of students, assuming that the traditional model must be bent to accomplish both the credentialling function demanded by the profession and the traditional, university demand for scholarship. Faculties of Education make little distinction in evaluating performance across a variety of needed, disparate roles.

The results of this dilemma are embarrassing to the professional faculty. Marshall Arlin of UBC noted in the late 1970s that for the total group of education professors at the associate level in Canada, in doctoral granting institutions, only about 26 per cent were pursuing careers committed to research scholarship.[4] Further, in Canada, 'fully 75 per cent of all the authors publishing educational articles in the past eight years have been one-study authors.'[5]

My point is a simple one. There can be no argument that faculty members are needed in Education whose primary function is practical, whose primary background is excellent performance and for whom publication and research is not a necessary condition. The fact that every single faculty in Canada has numbers of such people is in itself an empirical validation of this point. There is a problem if the same standards of performance are applied to this group as to experimental physicists. And this problem will inevitably arise if Faculties of Education do not differentiate roles and expectations.

At Simon Fraser University this problem was understood and solved from the moment the University opened its doors to students of teaching. The role of the Faculty Associate brings to our campus on term contract some of the best teachers in Canada. They carry out the essential, practical functions in close dialogue with the professoriate. While they do not carry the title or function of Professor, they are highly valued. The position — a seconded arrangement with school districts — is aggressively sought after. We have no disagreement with the rest of the university about the standards for tenure or promotion which apply to regular faculty. In fact the luxury of the associate program enables rigorous standards of research to be applied — we do not need the 'useful practitioner' in this tenurable group. More importantly, the fertilization of research in the faculty is stimulated by the yearly input of bright, enthusiastic practitioners.

Response

Consider, if you will, the statistics in Dr Birch's paper regarding SSHRC granting rates. What expectation would you have that the 28 regular faculty members at Simon Fraser University over the 5 years summarized would tie Alberta, double Calgary, triple Manitoba and double Western Ontario in grants received. Each of these institutions has substantially greater numbers of faculty. In two other studies of research productivity done in more recent years[6] which compared the rate per faculty member of refereed article output in a group of leading journals, Simon Fraser University led the entire group of education faculties in the country. There is no magic to this. It is simply that there ought to be a more rational approach to role assignments within the professional faculty. Valuable faculty members should be highly regarded in appropriate ways rather than forced to lie on procrustean beds. The ultimate result will be a more standard quality in the educational research effort emanating from Faculties of Education. While the current scene leaves something to be desired, there are opportunities for change. There are models to follow. 'The fault, dear Brutus...'.

Notes

[1] Science Council of Canada, *Science for Every Student: Educating Canadians for Tomorrow's World*, Report 36 (Hull, Quebec: Canadian Government Publishing Centre, April 1984).

[2] J.W. George Ivany and Michael E. Manley-Casimir (eds.), *Federal-Provincial Relations: Education Canada* (Toronto: OISE Press, 1981).

[3] Joseph J. Schwab, 'The Practical: A Language for Curriculum,' *School Review* (November 1969), pp. 1–23 and 'The Practical: Arts of the Eclectic,' *School Review* (August 1971), pp. 493–542.

[4] Marshall Arlin, 'Quantity and Impact of Scholarly Journal Publication in Canadian Faculties of Education,' *Canadian Journal of Education*, vol. 3 no. 1 (1978), p. 13.

[5] ... 'One-Study Publishing Typifies Educational Inquiry,' *Educational Researcher*, vol. 6 no. 9 (1977), p. 12.

[6] Philip Winne and Jack Martin, 'Research Productivity in Canadian Faculties of Education,' *CSSE News*, vol. 8 no. 3 (1981), pp. 3–5. and R.A. Clifton and N.G. McDonald, 'Research in Canadian Faculties of Education: Another Look,' *CSSE News*, vol. 11 no. 1 (1984), pp. 3–7.

5 The Contribution of Canadian Universities to Public Education

Bernard J. Shapiro

I welcome this opportunity to address the AUCC about a subject that I can only hope is of mutual interest.

In addressing this topic, I cannot pretend to bring to it the appropriate canons of scholarship, for I am not a historian. What I offer, therefore, is simply a comment based on the one hand on my reading and on the other hand on my experience in schools as a teacher, in universities as, successively, a researcher, a teacher and an administrator and, finally, in government as a freshman Deputy Minister.

Further, in my consideration of this topic, 'The Contribution of Canadian Universities to Public Education', I not only limit my consideration of education to schooling, but I further limit my definition of schooling to the elementary and secondary schools thus excluding the post-secondary sector which, in the Canadian context, is also publicly funded and forms an integral part of our arrangements for public schooling and, therefore, for public education.

The casual observer might expect to find strong links between the elementary and secondary schools on the one hand and the universities on the other. Not only do all of these institutions have the same patron, but they share the assumption that it is possible to improve our lives through the application of reason to the human condition. Further, and even more obviously, they are all in the teaching business — in fact serving many of the same people albeit at different points in their lives. It must, of course, be added that the research mission so fundamental to any useful conception of the university is not a characteristic of the elementary and the secondary schools. Nevertheless, more university graduates go into teaching than into any other single career. For example, 20.8 per cent of employed 1982 Ontario university graduates have entered teaching and related fields, surpassing the percentage attracted by any of the other twenty-two career groupings studied. Ontario's class of '82 produced more elementary school teachers than computer programmers. Is it not reasonable, therefore, to assume that universities would take a strong interest in the development of a schooling system which not only is the source of virtually all Canadian university students but is also the eventual employer of a substantial proportion of all Canadian university graduates?

Nearly a century ago, the president of the University of Chicago, William Rainey Harper, wrote, 'As a university, we are above all interested in pedagogy.' One might, indeed, think that this comment, expressing in its particular context the delight of President Harper in the arrival at the University of Chicago in 1894 of John Dewey, would, whatever its historical specificity, also ring true today.

I will, however, wish to argue that nothing could be further from the truth. Canadian universities, I would like to suggest, are quite naturally related to elementary and secondary schools in many ways. Further, Canadian universities both affect and are affected by, Canadian elementary and secondary schools. Nevertheless, I would assert that, allowing for some (although not many) individual exceptions, not only are Canadian universities not interested in pedagogy but that the contribution of Canadian universities to public schooling falls so far short of both these universities' possibilities and their responsibilities as to constitute something of a public scandal.

As part of my preparation for this afternoon's discussion and being particularly conscious of my taste for but lack of training in history, I reviewed (over a period of two decades) the minutes of the meetings of both the Council of Ontario Universities (COU) and the Association of Universities and Colleges of Canada (AUCC) in order to assess the extent to which issues concerning elementary and secondary schools were matters of recorded interest to either group. It appeared, at least from these minutes, that other than sporadic concern with and complaint about the achievement standards of secondary school graduates coming to university, elementary and secondary education seem rarely (and in one case, never) to have been discussed.

It was not always thus especially as regards public secondary schools. In fact, in Ontario, public secondary schools and public universities were joined at birth. In 1797, the Ontario Legislative Council petitioned the Crown for land grants to set up a grammar school in each district of the colony. This was coupled with a request for a similar grant to establish a college or university. This joining was, of course, a deliberate step. The secondary or grammar school was seen by those establishing it as a stepping-stone to the university, where the children of the establishment could enter the learned professions and join the establishment themselves. Thus, at the very beginning, the secondary school was seen (by both universities and the wider community) as a 'feeder' for the university even though only a small minority of the secondary or grammar school students actually went on to further education. Within this framework, however, it was both natural and appropriate to think of the Canadian system of formal schooling as essentially divided in two with the elementary schools (for the lower classes) on the one hand and both the secondary and university institutions (for the elite) on the other. Again within this initial framework, it made intuitive if not conceptual sense to organize the secondary school curriculum by academic discipline — in obvious preparation for and in pale reflection of the university degree programmes which lay ahead for a small but important student group.

Something, however, happened on the way to 1987. Responding to social, economic and political changes, the secondary schools became mass institutions to which all were not only admitted but, indeed, compelled to attend. Universities also expanded but to a much lesser extent. Thus, at present, the realities of selective admissions and established social status lead us to think of formal schooling as still divided into two sectors but now as between elementary and secondary schools (for the many) on the one hand and the post-secondary colleges and universities (still for the relatively few) on the other. It seems to me, however, that Canadian universities continue to relate to secondary schools as if the primary purpose of these schools was still to provide 'grist' (in the form of students as well as teaching or research assistants) for the 'university mill' (in the form of funded programmes). From the perspective of the Canadian establishment, this view has a certain appeal if only because we are ourselves the relatively successful products of the university education and screening system. For the majority of Canadians, however, and, more particularly, for the majority of young Canadians, this view bespeaks a kind of arrogance that is, unfortunately, reminiscent of the 'hubris' associated with some of the figures of great or even not-so-great Greek tragedy. In fact, however, the secondary schools in Canada are multi-purpose institutions from which more students go directly to work than to post-secondary programmes at either the college or the university level. The potential contribution of our universities to the modern secondary school remains as great if not greater than it ever was. This contribution remains, however, more potential than real. The universities' original contribution to the secondary schools (the organization of the curriculum by academic discipline) has long since out-lived its usefulness. Their continuing contribution of a standard of perform-ance to which both schools and students are expected to rise is, I believe, of substantial value. One might wish, however, that this standard was less variable than is evidenced by these universities' rather flexible approach to admission standards (these standards seem to vary more reliably with enrolment targets than with performance criteria) or that the standard could be more interestingly varied so that new images of the future could be held up to those students not likely to participate in university life directly.

If the universities' potential with regard to the public secondary schools remains largely unrealized, it, nevertheless, looms large in com-parison to the universities' contributions to the public elementary schools. With elementary as opposed to secondary schools, the historical link is missing; the relatively populist nature of the enterprise runs up against the more elitist conception of higher education (indeed, until relatively recently, university spokespersons were more likely to oppose rather than favour the extension of elementary and secondary schooling); and there are, of course, neither the opportunities nor the problems presented by a student interface as between the two institutions.

It is, I must add, not only a question of the relative egocentrism of the universities as institutions. This is, I believe, a part of the difficulty, but there is something else as well. Although both public schools and universities are teaching institutions, public schools are primarily and, indeed, almost exclusively devoted to teaching whereas universities are centres of both teaching and research. Indeed, I understand the special genius of universities to be that wonderful, if not always realized, synergy of instruction and inquiry, of pedagogy and the generation of new knowledge and understanding. This difference need not, however, have been crucial with respect to the contribution of Canadian universities to public schools (the knowledge produced by universities could, after all, be very useful to schools) if Canadian universities actually were (as was William Rainey Harper) interested in pedagogy.

Unfortunately, although with some quite fascinating exceptions, this has not generally been the case. University curricula are organized around research and not teaching paradigms; talk about teaching in faculty lounges is much more likely to reflect an indirect admission of research plans going awry than it is to reflect a substantial interest in teaching itself; and what is more vulnerable during periods of budget constraint than the university offices of instructional development? What this represents (less markedly, it is true, in those of the university programmes that are directed at vocations outside of the university itself) is not any lack of commitment by the universities to the importance or the value of teaching. Partly it represents the apparent accessibility of the teaching role to amateurs so that teachers, the occupiers of this role at whatever level of the system, can never be seen as more than members of what Etzioni calls a 'semi-profession.' More importantly, it represents the easy if unwarranted assumption not only that teaching is an art (after all, even the arts can be cultivated) but also that teaching arises as a natural consequence of subject matter knowledge. Pedagogy is not a legitimate concern inside university Ph.D. programmes not because it is seen as unimportant but simply because it is believed (ironically in the face of overpowering contrary evidence at the universities themselves) that complex knowledge provides both the necessary and the sufficient basis for complex and competent teaching.

I accept, indeed, I embrace, the universities' view that subject matter knowledge is necessary for effective teaching and to the limited extent that this has led us to require appropriate academic background for public school teachers, the contribution of Canadian universities to public schools is both acknowledged and appreciated. Such subject matter knowledge is not, however, sufficient to effective teaching, and the continuing notion that it is has led to a prior and unfortunate limitation on the contribution that universities could be making to the public schools. Thus it is, for example, that the universities focus on secondary schools and the secondary school teachers rather than on elementary schools and elementary school teachers. Secondary school teachers had 'real' knowledge to deal with and were seen as needing, therefore, some university training — although not, in the first instance, the full degree treatment. The elementary school teachers, on the other hand, given the 'simple' subject matter involved, could be relegated to what was seen to be the less demanding environment of the normal school and even that institution was regarded by many as superfluous.

The issue of the normal school and, therefore, of teacher education, is, perhaps, the ground on which my relatively negative view of the contribution of Canadian universities to public schools can best be challenged. After all, not a few Canadian universities and many Canadian Faculties of Education were originally either normal schools or other free-standing teacher training institutions — a fact not often featured in the current brochures of these same universities. Further, all Canadian public school teachers are university graduates, thus assuring that the profession is composed of educated men and women at least to the extent that Canadian universities are effectively dealing with their responsibilities in general or liberal education. Most importantly of all, almost all Canadian universities are actively involved in teacher education. Most have Faculties or Departments of Education some with both graduate and undergraduate programmes. Moreover, even those Faculties of Education without graduate programmes are also involved with — indeed sometimes enjoy a public monopoly over — recognized professional development programmes for practising educators. In other words, Canadian universities now house all three dimensions of teacher education — academic, professional and continuing education. How well is this arrangement working? Has it achieved the expected results in terms of better teachers and ultimately — whether through better teachers and/or surer knowledge from research a better quality of education for Canadian children?

In some ways, I believe that the answers to these questions can be positive and affirming relative to the universities' contribution to public schooling. Although most general education programmes at Canadian universities are not, in my view, sufficient to the responsibilities of Canadian universities in this regard, I do believe that the universities provide both a context and a substance of learning much more appropriate and much more adequate than that which would be available in free-standing professional institutions. Thus, as Canada has moved from a situation in which only some of its public school teachers were university educated to a situation in which virtually all Canadian teachers are university educated, I believe that the general quality of teachers and their teaching has improved and that, therefore, there has been a significant increase in the value (albeit unmeasured) of the education offered in our elementary and secondary schools.

Moving from the contribution of the universities with regard to general education to the contribution of the universities with regard to professional education, the situation becomes a good deal more complex. The relationship between Faculties of Education and the universities of which they are a part has always been and continues to be uneasy. The prestige of the teaching profession (probably one of the reasons that the organized profession sought university affiliation) is not high at least as compared, for example, to law or to medicine. Further, many university faculties continue to be of the opinion that 'education' lacks the discipline, the research knowledge and the theoretical base that would make it a topic suitable for university study. Finally, many practising educators (some of the best of whom were recruited to the university Faculties of Education) failed to see what the university connection added to the value of these same educators' own thoughtful experience in regard to the preparation of the next generation of teachers. Thus, from the very beginning, the relationship between Faculties of Education and the larger university was often less a question of love at first sight than an example of a shotgun marriage — often imposed by the provincial government in the perhaps unaccustomed role of the outraged but sometimes generous parent.

The general difficulty with shotgun marriages, however, is that one reaps neither the advantages of free love nor the consolations of the more conventionally sanctified arrangements. Specifically with regard to professional education, the result in most, although not all, cases has been the isolation of the Faculties of Education and, therefore, of the teacher education programmes within the very universities of which they are nominally a part. Neither the theory nor the practical knowledge of the university community seems generally available to its Faculty of Education. Similarly, neither the practical experience nor the theoretical knowledge of the Faculty of Education seems generally available to the rest of the university community. Each group manages quite effectively to be disdainful of the other (often for the very same reasons), and neither seems to have been concerned with the extent to which each is thereby a loser. It is, however, clear to both which side has the higher status in the university pecking order. In this scheme of things, the Faculty of Education is generally somewhere down near the bottom along with, perhaps, nursing, forestry, and social work.

Despite these difficulties, some of the outcomes have been worthwhile. Faculties of Education (and to some degree their parent universities) can take the credit for new and consistently increasing levels of educational research activity within the Faculties themselves — and to some lesser extent within other university departments. Further, Faculties of Education can draw considerable satisfaction from both the increasing range in the models of professional preparation now available and the faculties' major contribution to the markedly increased professional capabilities of practising educators. There are, however, two difficulties. First, these admittedly positive outcomes have not been either as marked or as widespread as had been anticipated. Second, they were often accomplished in spite of the university environment rather than because of it, and I would suggest that the responsibility for this result lies at least in some major way with the narrowness of the universities' own conception of their role and their mission with regard to our elementary and secondary schools. *Noblesse oblige* is all very well in its own way, but it is certainly no substitute for what has really been needed from the universities, and that is a substantive commitment. Given the rhetoric from government, from the profession and from the universities themselves, one might have expected some evidence that the universities would accord the future of the public schools a high priority not so much in terms of student revenue as in the attempt to bring the wide ranging resources of the university to bear on both the understanding and the future of these central social institutions. I still await the day. Perhaps, this is, in fact, the day.

In the meantime, in response to their relative isolation within university institutions, Canadian Faculties of Education have, in many cases attempted to take on the characteristics of the more established university departments. How else, for example, can one explain the apparent determination of Faculties to define all relevant professional development for teachers in terms of university degree credits — generally at the graduate level? Similarly, how else can one explain the tendency to formulate, within Faculties of Education, research questions more easily related to particular academic disciplines than to problems of professional practice and conundrums of professional experience. The result has generally been disastrous like that of any all too-human failure of nerve. Not only are we often treated to second-rate philosophy, history, psychology and sociology — this, after all, is also characteristic of the standard academic departments, but in relationship to the Faculties of Education, this is often achieved at the expense of what would have been first-rate curriculum theory and other concerns basic to the experience and the needs of the reflective classroom practitioner. The further unwelcome consequence of such chameleon-like behaviour is an increasing estrangement of the Faculties of Education not only from their university but also from their professional colleagues. Thus, from a societal point of view, or, perhaps, it is just from the point of view of an untried and untested civil servant, the hope that the association of professional education with our universities would lead not only to better professional training but also to a more usefully cumulative body of knowledge relevant to policy choices for the country's schools than would otherwise have been the case has remained, especially with regard to policy issues, unrealized and unfulfilled. The interest of the wider university community has apparently not been piqued.

From a certain perspective, this problem can, at least in principle, be easily resolved. I can, perhaps, best describe this perspective in terms of my current experience as Deputy Minister of Education for the Province of Ontario. As part of what I understand to be my responsibilities in this new role, I spend four days a month sitting in the back of elementary and secondary school classrooms in order to provide for myself some concrete referent for the policy development exercise which is my major responsibility at the Ministry. Part of the continuing surprise of these school visits is the extent to which I find that imaginative teachers and other school personnel have, in fact, resolved thorny issues of professional practice — issues still being hotly and often fruitlessly debated either in the so-called corridors of power or, for that matter, in the groves of academe. The difficulty is that these local resolutions are not generally known beyond the local jurisdiction and may even be confined to a specific local teacher or classroom. Further, these model practices are generally more intuitively than conceptually understood, and little thought at all has usually been given to either their generalizability and/or their dissemination. It seems to me that this presents a golden and continuing opportunity to the universities at large and to the Faculties of Education in particular. Which of these models can be conceptually grounded? Which can be generalized and to what extent? How can the resources of mind and technique resident in the university community be used not only so as to refine and better articulate the practical operation but also to suggest new and possibly more powerful ways in which to proceed?

In this context, where are the university laboratory schools? Where are the demonstration schools operated jointly by local boards and Faculties of Education? Where are the guidelines for the application of new knowledge to the realities of professional practice? Where are the communication vehicles that translate the reconstructed logic of the academic journal for the benefit of those (whether in the schools and/or in government) that should be encouraged to make tomorrow's decisions on a basis of an understanding more perfect than today's? It is a quarter century since we benefitted from Northrop Frye's *Designs for Learning*. How much longer must we wait?

This is, as I have suggested, an opportunity for Canadian universities (hopefully through both their Faculties of Education and the broader range of university departments) to greatly increase their work with and contribution to public schooling through the elucidation, conceptualization and, where appropriate, generalization of professional practice. To be effective, however, this theory/practice nexus must, of course, be thought of as a two-way street. It is not a question of either understanding theory so as to modify practice or a question of observing practice so as to modify theoretical understanding. Both these questions must be addressed simultaneously, for in any one instance or on any one day, who is to say whether the insight will be one of professional practice suggesting new theoretical parameters, or perhaps, the other way around?

Interestingly enough, the professional resolutions that I reported seeing in our elementary and secondary schools are often also visible in Canadian Faculties of Education. It is not difficult for me to point to particularly imaginative and apparently productive approaches to both teacher training and, to a lesser extent, educational research whether at the University of British Columbia, Simon Fraser, Lethbridge or Toronto, to suggest only a few possibilities. The irony in the university context is that these ventures (inside institutions devoted to research and, therefore, committed to the testing of their work in the wider colleague community) frequently remain as unknown and, therefore, as undeveloped as do their counterparts in the local school districts. One need not think of radical steps. It would be progress enough, perhaps, if the faculties who have developed their programmes could, with or without the assistance of other university colleagues, more usually cast these programmes in a research mode in an effort to assess their outcomes, establish their generalizability and then bend every effort to both test and establish this knowledge in the public domain.

The elaboration of educational 'praxis' whether in faculties or in schools is only the most obvious of the challenges facing a university and a profession that are concerned to contribute together to the future of public education. Related to but not either quite parallel or quite orthogonal to these concerns is the arena of policy studies. Although new in the role of Deputy Minister, I find myself, not surprisingly, faced with a range of policy problems which must be addressed in the relatively near-term future. These policy questions range from the ridiculous to the sublime. Ignoring both ends of this continuum, some of the issues which I am currently grappling within the policy area are: high school drop-outs; the management of the transition from school to work; literacy failures in both adult and elementary school programmes; the relationship between equality (of opportunity) and excellence (in performance); the consequences of various taxation models for the Province's schools; the value and place of religious and moral education in publicly funded institutions; the role of secondary schools in adult and continuing education; the relationship between multiculturism and school languages of instruction, etc. etc. These and many other questions are of some importance relative to the future of public education, but my experience with the universities as sources for assistance in understanding and dealing with these issues is not a happy one. It is not that university personnel are unwilling to make themselves available as consultants or that the universities and Faculty of Education talent pool is basically inadequate. Rather, it is my experience that the talent pool is too highly specialized. Even more importantly the talent pool is all too often made up of the experience of appropriate colleague relationships in what are (from a policy although not necessarily from an academic perspective) related areas of expertise. What I would, therefore, call for, from those of you who have a substantial interest in the contribution of universities to public education is the development of centres for policy studies that have special salience for our elementary and secondary schools. As in any other area of policy work, these centres, if they are to be useful, would have to be sufficiently catholic in their tastes to bring together expertise and experience from a variety of academic and professional sources. Such centres might, however, be one way in which the isolation of professional education at Canadian universities could be reduced with the result, I believe, of not only a more valuable contribution of Canadian universities to public education but also a new and intellectually productive venture for both my colleagues in our Faculties of Education and those in other university schools and departments.

At the Ontario Ministry of Education, we attempt to scan the future with regard to the public schools. The first round of this scanning exercise has suggested to us a future in which the Ministry will continue to use its fiscal resources to leverage its point of view into actual practice but that the Ministry's focus of attention will shift from program development and program delivery to policy development on the one hand and on the other hand the elaborate negotiation of program delivery with a set of local institutions much wider than the current set of school boards. We are anxious to test this idea and this image of the future against the minds and the expertise of those of our university colleagues both inside and outside of the Faculties of Education willing to devote time and imagination to the task. I can only hope the universities will be not only willing but anxious to respond.

It is not only the universities who must act. The Government, the private sector and, indeed, the schools themselves have unmet responsibilities. Nevertheless, my point of view suggests, as I am sure you are already aware, not only that I believe that the universities can make an important contribution to public education but that they ought to do so — that such a commitment is, in fact, inherent in the very idea of a university. An opposite argument certainly could be made, one that would focus on the universities' responsibilities to, for example, both knowledge and social criticism. The development of knowledge and the role and responsibility of social critic are, in my view, necessary for the future of both the universities and the wider society. They are not, however, sufficient at least for the universities. My image of the university is not that of a twentieth century monastery but that of a twentieth century cathedral. *Pace*, Cardinal Newman.

In the famous children's fairy tale of *Snow White and the Seven Dwarfs*, the wicked stepmother gazes into her magic mirror and asks,

Mirror, mirror on the wall
Who is the fairest of us all?

My hope for the future is that this question does not capture the nature of the universities' intended relationship to public education. If it did, it would suggest that the universities are so self-absorbed as to be satisfied with constantly holding up mirrors to themselves and considering public education only insofar as these schools are reflected in that very special but often narrow silvered glass.

Response

George E. Connell

I would like to begin by saying that when the idea for this conference was suggested, I immediately welcomed the opportunity to participate in a program designed to encourage my colleagues in university administration, members of Faculties of Education and government representatives to address what is a timely concern for us all: the need to regard public education as a collective responsibility. Academic collaboration is a fundamental key to educational reform.

Pressures for Re-thinking Canadian Universities' Contribution to Public Education

At the heart of our shared concern for the future of public education in Canada (and by that I mean education as defined by government and funded by government) is, I believe, an ill-defined relationship between universities, Faculties of Education and the Ministry of Education.

In the United States, the current teacher education reform movement was sparked four years ago by the report of the National Commission on Excellence in Education, *A Nation at Risk*, which raised critical questions about the quality of public education. 1986 saw the publication of two more influential reports, *Tomorrow's Teachers* by the Holmes Group and *A Nation Prepared* from the Carnegie Task Force on Teaching as a Profession. Each of the reports identified major concerns with the schools and the teacher education process; more importantly, however, they addressed social trends, the changing goals of education and the need to develop a more advanced educational system.

In Canada, interest has also been expressed in reform, notably in Alberta and in Ontario. Here in Ontario I would draw your attention to the Position Paper, *Teacher Education in Ontario: Current Practice and Options for the Future* (1987) and two reports which prompted the current Ministry review of teacher education, *Future Directions in Preservice*

Teacher Education in Ontario (Ontario Association of Deans, 1983) and *Response to Ontario Association of Deans of Education Submission* (Council of Ontario Universities, Special Committee on Teacher Education, 1984).

The authors of the Position Paper, Professors Michael Fullan and Michael Connelly, assert that the pressures and needs for reform are various. I shall identify three of them that interest me in particular:

(a) The ambiguity in the role of Faculties of Education, torn between the demands of scholarship and those of the field, operating with overloaded agendas and limited resources.

(b) Problems in the enhancement of the profession of teaching, both at the school and the university levels. At the school level the central issue is the development of a thinking skilled, effective profession of teachers. Within universities, the status of faculties and their abilities to relate equally and effectively to both university and field are at stake.

(c) The opportunity for reform, given retirement patterns in school boards and in faculty positions at the university level; and the likelihood of cooperation among the major educational partners: government, boards, teacher federations, administrative officials, universities.[1]

To the list, our recent experience with the schools in Ontario compels me to add a fourth important pressure for reform; the need for curricular coherence, or vertical integration of the curriculum from primary school to secondary school to university. The Position Paper concludes its call for reform by saying we in Ontario must 'create a new model for teacher education, one that will demand major changes to the current system of teacher preparation.'[2]

I find this challenge to create a new, innovative model for education in Ontario, especially if it is to be founded on the cooperation of all partners in the education enterprise, an exciting one, and one which I am prepared to commit my faculty to.

Current research in learning theory stresses the importance of the continuity of the learning process. In his address to a 1980 conference on higher education, Ernest Boyer, president of the Carnegie Foundation for the Advancement of Teaching, identified this continuity and expressed the need to move in the direction of closer cooperation between secondary and post-secondary teachers: 'In recent years,' Boyer said, 'the relationship between the colleges and schools has been essentially ignored. Presidents and Deans refuse to talk to Principals and District Superintendents. College faculty refuse to meet with their counterparts in the public schools. And curriculum reforms at each level are planned in total isolation.'[3] I would argue that the situation in Canada is not as dire as the one described by Dr

Boyer, but it is nevertheless true that the transition from secondary school has not received the attention that it deserves.

The gap between universities and schools has occasionally been bridged. Professor Robin Harris reminded me recently of the establishment in November 1960 of the Joint Committee of the University of Toronto and the Toronto Board of Education at the request of the Board to address, in particular, the then pressing question of curriculum revision, in addition to matters concerning admission and general liaison. This was the first occasion that a board of education and a university had together and as equal partners made a joint study of the curriculum. Influenced by Jerome Bruner, the committee adopted as its premise the view that 'education is a process, that each subject is a continuum and the development of ideas or concepts, not the absorption of facts, must inform the course of study from the first grade to graduate school.'[4]

The Joint Committee's work resulted in the publication in 1962 of the influential book *Design for Learning*. The work, edited by the then Principal of Victoria College, Northrop Frye, consisted of three reports prepared jointly by teachers from the Toronto public and secondary schools and University of Toronto professors. The key recommendation was establishment of an Institute of Curricular Research and Development in Ontario. [This of course, formed the blueprint for the Ontario Institute for Studies in Education (OISE).] This recommendation took as its premise that reform of the curriculum demands the combined efforts of teachers from all levels, and, as Professor Harris then stressed, this cannot be achieved unless there is 'active and imaginative collaboration between boards of education and universities and between both boards and universities and the Ministry of Education on one hand and the Teachers' Federation on the other.'[5] To the collaborative enterprise, I would, however, add a critically important fourth dimension or partnership — the relationship between Faculties of Education and the universities of which they are a part.

The Report of the Special Committee on Teacher Education (COU, 1984) chaired by Bernard Shapiro, made the following observation,

> It is now over fifteen years since Ontario's teacher education programs were placed within the Province's universities. The expectations at the time related partly to status considerations but much more importantly to the hope that the emerging relationship between the Faculties of Education and other university units would develop in a way beneficial to the teacher education program. In some cases this development has, no doubt, occurred; in others, it may not have, leaving the larger university community and the Faculty of Education relatively isolated with respect to each other.[6]

The history of teacher training programs in Ontario helps to make the current situation understandable. Until 1965, the Ministry of Education presided over all pre- and in-service teacher education programs. Normal schools (renamed Teacher Colleges in 1953) were directly managed by the Ministry of Education; admission standards and program content were fully controlled by the Minister; and the Principals of the colleges were appointed by him. The teaching staff were civil servants. The situation at the Ontario College of Education was similar. Although nominally attached since 1920 to the University of Toronto, Government influence on the general shape of the program was strong.

In response to the McLeod Committee which had been established to recommend improvements in what was 'widely felt to be an unsatisfactory training system for teachers'[7], in March 1966 the Minister of Education announced the transfer of the major responsibility for teacher education to the universities with the intention of improving program quality. Adjustment to the transfer, which was not completely accomplished until 1972, proved to be uneasy: for its part the Ministry of Education was reluctant to relinquish its control and fears were expressed by the profession that in a university setting, teacher education would become less practical, less field-based and overly theoretical in emphasis. The universities expressed concern about 'having to accept, without exception, the college staffs, who were, in many cases, not academically qualified to teach in the universities.'[8] These feelings are not fully resolved today.

Unlike other university faculties, including the professional ones, the Ministry of Education controls admission requirements of candidates to Faculties of Education through Regulation 269, 'Ontario's Teacher's Qualifications.' Part I of the Regulation defines the qualifications needed to become a teacher in Ontario, and in general terms, prescribes the curriculum for Faculties of Education.

The basic mandate of Faculties of Education in Ontario today is therefore to prepare its teaching candidates according to Ministry of Education requirements so they are eligible to receive an Ontario Teaching Certificate and a Bachelor of Education degree. But the Ministry of Education has done considerably more than determine a mandate for the Faculties of Education. It has in fact largely prescribed, sometimes in unusual programmatic detail, how the Faculties of Education should carry out their mandate. I can think of no other faculty in my own university or any other which has had so much of its curriculum determined externally. Dr Shapiro observes that it was the universities' sense of academic disciplines that determined a large part of the secondary school curriculum. That may be true, but if it is, the Ministry of Education has been a willing and even enthusiastic promoter of the idea, and has virtually institutionalized it in the domination that it exerts over Faculties of Education. On their parts, the universities and the Faculties of Education have not advanced firm alternatives to the Ministry's initiatives. Perhaps if we did, the Ministry might feel less compelled to prescribe how and what prospective teachers will be taught, and to set so explicitly the agendas for educational research.

The fact that Faculties of Education are too often on the periphery of their universities suggests to me that universities have not had as much influence on secondary education as Dr Shapiro claims. The Ministry's influence, however, is obvious and profound. The fit between Ministry regulations and our BEd programs is almost perfect. New developments are almost always restricted to disjointed 'special initiatives' in various areas which, although momentarily important, often turn out to be ephemeral.

In funding the research that could lead to the sort of reform for which Dr Shapiro calls, the Government of Ontario has taken the unusual step of separating its major investment from not only the Faculties of Education but to a significant extent from the universities as well. The Ministry's major investment in research is made at The Ontario Institute for Studies in Education (OISE). Research is the prime mover towards change. But the Ministry's present concentration of support for research does not encourage change.

Where there has been a modicum of change initiated within universities (for example in the introduction of MA (T) and MSc (T), degrees) the Ministry's and the federations' response has been remarkably cool. And when the Ministry does not respond with approbation and support, the boards of education are equally cool.

I would ask the same question that Dr Shapiro did about laboratory schools: where are they? There are two at the University of Toronto. But the Ministry's interest in them has been at best indifferent. The same can be said about the absence of policy development which Dr Shapiro, I think correctly, laments. But again I see little support from his Ministry for a comprehensive educational research strategy that would lead to new policies and the development of policy expertise.

Understanding this tension allows us to formulate an effective proposal for change. I hasten to add, however, that I do not necessarily regard as incompatible the universities' and the Ministry's demands on Faculties of Education. I am of the view that Faculties of Education should 'stick to their knitting' by teaching potential teachers how to teach and do so in a manner informed by both research and practice. As a corollary the universities must help them establish more formal cooperative links with other university faculties and departments to give complementary depth in academic subject areas (for example, the MA/MSc (T) program at the University of Toronto does this very well). What the faculties themselves must do is describe how they wish to go about their business. Removal of constraints will not automatically produce change. The Ministry and the universities can do no more than provide and support an opportunity for change. The Faculties of Education must decide how they will use that opportunity.

During the last twenty years some professional faculties in Canadian universities have gone through a profound change. Faculties of Law, for example, have broken free of a narrow definition of the requirements of legal education. They have expanded their research repertory beyond doctrinal analysis to explore the foundations of jurisprudence in history and philosophy, and to build bridges to scholars in economics, commerce, politics, sociology and psychology. They are certain to have a much more creative role in the legal system and in public affairs in the future.

Perhaps the time is ripe for a parallel breakthrough in Faculties of Education. The universities should be vigilant in order to ensure that truly seminal initiatives are recognized and properly nourished.

Notes

[1] M. Fullan and F.M. Connelly, *Teacher Education in Ontario: Current Practice and Options for the Future* (Toronto: Ministry of Education/Ministry of Colleges and Universities, 1987), pp. 6–7.

[2] *Ibid.*, p. 7.

[3] Ron Fortune, 'School-College Collaboration Programs in English' in Joseph Gibaldi (ed.), *Options for Teaching* (Chicago: Modern Language Association of America, 1986), Introduction.

[4] Robin Harris, 'Curriculum Research in Ontario,' An address to the Victoria College Women's Association, Toronto, 1962, p. 10.

[5] *Ibid.*, p. 2.

[6] Council of Ontario Universities, *Report of the Special Committee on Teacher Education* (Toronto: COU, 1984), p. 5.

[7] Fullan and Connelly, *op. cit.*, p. 11.

[8] *Ibid.*

Response

Nancy M. Sheehan

Several weeks ago on my way to the University of British Columbia I had a conversation with a cab driver, a young man in his mid-twenties, which went something like this:

Driver:	Do you work at the University?
Sheehan:	Yes!
Driver:	What do you do there?
Sheehan:	I'm a Professor.
Driver:	Does that mean that you teach?
Sheehan:	Yes, I teach.
Driver:	What do you teach?
Sheehan:	Er, I'm in education! (At times like this it would be so much simpler to say math, or engineering or English)
Driver:	What does that mean, education?
Sheehan:	That means I teach teachers!
Driver:	You mean teachers need to be taught! You mean they don't just stand up there and teach?

This anecdote neatly sums up one of the themes Dr Shapiro raises in his chapter, 'The Contribution of Canadian Universities to Public Education,' and perhaps explains why he calls the university input to public education 'a public scandal.'

Public school teachers haven't always had to be taught to teach and, as Shapiro points out, universities still assume that knowledge of the subject matter is enough to teach in the university. The notion that teachers needed more than subject matter knowledge developed with the establishment of mass schooling in the nineteenth century. With common schools for all came public financing, control and accountability. To ensure that the public was getting its money's worth and that there was some standard among teachers, Normal Schools were established to train the teachers and ensure the taxpayer that the teachers were competent.[1]

As the notion of mass schooling became accepted the public schools began to expand in the numbers and kinds of courses offered, in the length of the school day and year and in the kinds of students attracted to them. Over the years the high schools, academic to begin with, changed to accommodate a changing clientele and a changing climate. The early high schools had close links with the universities. As Shapiro relates not only were high schools organized by academic discipline but university professors sat on provincial examination committees, they authored school textbooks and the offerings of the high school remained closely tied to the universities' entrance requirements.

Beginning in 1945 in Alberta, Normal Schools began to become part of universities. What, in retrospect, should have been an opportunity for the universities to have an even greater influence on public schooling had the opposite effect. Shapiro equates this to the lack of satisfaction of a shotgun marriage. Normal schools were not welcomed with open arms by universities — one year programs, lower entrance requirements and instructors whose credentials were less than those of most professors did not help. The resulting low status on campus; a lack of institutional support — moral, if not financial; no attempt to understand or recognize professional responsibilities or activity; and an arts/science standard for all did not help integrate Faculties of Education into the academic life of the university. The resulting isolation and the notion that education faculties were the liaison between the public school system and the university meant that the rest of the institution has excluded itself from involvement with the schools for the most part.

Despite the claim by both the university and the Faculty of Education that the whole institution is involved in teacher education Shapiro's point that pedagogy is not of concern in the university is a valid one. He argues however, that in the area of subject matter knowledge for secondary teachers, universities have played an important role. I would suggest that the lack of interest in pedagogy within the university affects the preparation of secondary teachers in both subject matter content and in teaching skills. Let me give some examples.

At the University of Calgary we have developed a program of joint degrees — five year BEd/BSc or BEd/BA degrees for the education of science teachers or English teachers, etc. To us these programs have several advantages over both the four-year Bachelor of Education degree and the certification program for holders of first degrees. After we had received university approval for the first of these the Faculty of Humanities asked if we would be willing to devise a five-year joint degree with them for French teachers. We formed a committee of members from both education and humanities and met to work out the details. As we began to talk about core French, French immersion, and first-language French teachers there were protests from the French representatives. When I explained that we needed a program to provide teachers who taught in French as well as the French language the comment was: 'That's your problem, that's got nothing to do with us!' In the same vein most science faculties are oriented by discipline, and preparation for graduate school is their focus. The report of the Science Council of Canada, *Science for Every Student*, advocates that high school science courses be technology driven, integrative rather than discipline oriented and should focus on issues.[2] Science faculties which provide the subject matter preparation for teachers seem unaware that the high school teacher must cater to a broad range of students, that discipline-based instruction is not central to high school courses and that issues related to technology must be addressed.

It somehow seems ironic to me that the universities which are responsible for teacher education, complain that the schools produce graduates who cannot write and rather arrogantly impose 'effective writing exams,' not once asking themselves what their role might be in this failure in the public system. Could it be that teachers with majors in English literature have had few courses in composition, history of the language and linguistics? Could it be that these teachers find English literature more interesting than teaching composition? Certainly most English departments do not offer a lot of courses in such areas nor do they tend to specialize in children's literature. Courses on topics that appeal to adolescents, like science fiction, fantasy, the short story, even the modern Canadian novel are not generally promoted by university departments of English.

The attitude common in universities that subject matter knowledge is sufficient preparation to teach at the university level affects the preparation of secondary teachers since high schools have traditionally been organized by academic discipline. This is evident in the preference given to the consecutive (BEd after a first degree) as opposed to the concurrent (four year BEd) certification program.[3] This may also explain the widespread belief that those with a first degree can learn in a period not to exceed one academic year various teaching methodologies; understand child development; recognize children with special needs; obtain evaluation, classroom management and discipline skills; have practice teaching experience in classrooms; understand how schools function and adapt their discipline oriented background to the integrated orientation of the schools.[4]

These examples all relate to the university's role in the education of teachers. However, changes in access, in lifelong education and in technology suggest that what goes on in the public system should be of concern to the institutions beyond their teacher preparation role.

Access

Since the university no longer has entrance examinations we rely on the school system to establish a standard. If half of the students who have university entrance qualifications in mathematics fail to perform satisfactorily in the first year mathematics courses, that should be of concern.

Financially, psychologically, and socially this affects the students, the university and the society. Instead of *blaming* the schools, surely even acquainting the schools with these statistics would be a start. The schools have no way of knowing what happens to their graduates. In times of scarce resources everyone involved in education must cooperate to make sure the best use is being made of our human potential.

Lifelong Education

Because the university population is no longer only 18–24 year olds, and no longer only full-time students for four years the university must adapt its offerings to meet these changes. Innovative ways of handling on-going education must be implemented: in-service courses, part-time graduate programs, outreach offerings, courses by teleconferencing, Spring/Summer sessions, study at home and by television are some of these. These structural and instructional changes, although often pushed for by Faculties of Education, may need to become the standard across the campus if the university is to retain any credibility as an educational institution. Already, corporations, companies, private institutes, etc. offer courses; in the United States some even offer degrees. Major companies assume many of their personnel will spend a day each week learning. Universities must be flexible to adapt to changing needs and possibilities and to compete with the competition. In the process they may learn from Faculties of Education for whom the on-going education of the teacher has long been a concern.[5]

Technological Revolution

Students who have spent their childhood and adolescence in front of a computer, in a video games centre or watching science fiction on television find themselves in large lecture theatres absorbing content — sometimes outdated, regurgitating that content and perhaps learning that hand-held memory calculators cannot be used in the examination. Students brought up on technology are told that technology cannot be used! What kind of a message are we delivering to these students — that the university instead of being in the forefront of change is actually preserving and entrenching the status quo? It reminds me of the public school regulation that did not allow the use of ball-point pens when they were first introduced because they would encourage sloppiness. As if the scratchy nibs and ink blots were examples of neatness!

If the university is to have a major effect on society then part of what it must do is understand that society. The public education system not only supplies the university with the majority of its students, it is also a microcosm of the society. It accepts all children, from the severely handicapped, those with great talent, and members of all ethnic, religious and political groups to those in the remotest northern and isolated communities and in the ghettos of our largest cities. The university should be able to learn from and in turn affect the public education system. But to do so it must change its image of neglect of the public schools. That will not be an easy task.

First of all it means keeping up to date with the system itself, reading about and analysing the public school process. Mostly this is done now by people in Faculties of Education. But surely mathematicians, scientists, specialists in English and history should know how their subject areas are being handled in the schools.

Second, it may mean serving on committees. This can be very time-consuming and not so easy to arrange. Alberta Education is undertaking a major revision of the high school curriculum. One of the areas affected is mathematics. I asked Alberta Education to ask the head of our mathematics department to sit on the Mathematics Curriculum Committee and I persuaded him to accept. He has been complaining for years about the inadequate mathematics background of the high school students and Alberta Education has been arguing that mathematics was being used inappropriately as a selector to most programs and faculties. I don't know what the outcome will be but it has to be better than if the liaison had not occurred.

Third, we should apply the findings of social science research to the university. We have many researchers who study children, the school, the family, and the society from which the high school graduates are coming. Does any of this research impact the workings of the university? We need to use the findings of this research to adapt university instruction, content and process to the changing culture of the society.

Fourth, to make the research known and understood to those in the university and the school system who can benefit from it, it must be disseminated in such a way that university administrators and faculty, teachers, curriculum makers and school administrators can benefit. As Shapiro points out this is not the refereed article in an exclusive academic journal. The research must be reported in readily understood language, in a publication available to teachers, and in a style that shows its applicability to the classroom. For this to happen the university must adapt its reward criteria so that this kind of work is compensated, something Faculties of Education and other professional faculties have been struggling with for years.

Fifth, Shapiro calls for the development of centres for policy studies related to the public schools. I would expand this to interdisciplinary research centres in all areas connected with public education. It would be a way of getting around our departmental/faculty structure, of acknowledging that the whole university is concerned about public education and the education of techers, of providing a ready source of, and outlet for, applied research, and of enabling faculty members from a variety of disciplines to benefit from one another. In the end the result could be an institution which better understands its students, the changing society and the technology to which they have been exposed. It may help establish an atmosphere of mutual respect, not only between the university and the public education system but also between Faculties of Education and the rest of the university.

Notes

[1]See, for example, J. Donald Wilson *et. al.*, (eds.), *Canadian Education: A History* (Scarborough: Prentice Hall, 1970), p. 220 and George S. Tomkins, *A Common Countenance: Stability and Change in the Canadian Curriculum* (Scarborough: Prentice Hall, 1986), pp. 71–73.

[2]Science Council of Canada, *Science for Every Student: Educating Canadians for Tomorrow's World* Report 36 (Hull, Quebec: Canadian Government Publishing Centre, 1984).

[3]The University of Calgary, *The Shrinking Maze: Report of the University Program Review Committee* (Calgary: The University of Calgary, 1980), p. 98.

[4]The University of British Columbia, *Background to and Rationale for the Revised Teacher Education Program* (Vancouver: Faculty of Education, Internal Document 1986).

[5]See, for example, K. Patricia Cross, 'New Students in New Bottles,' in A.W. Neilsen and Chad Gaffield, *Universities in Crisis: A Medieval Institution in the Twenty-first Century* (Montreal: Institute for Research on Public Policy, 1986), pp. 215–230 and Thomas H.B. Symons, 'Canadian Post-secondary Education: The Cultural Agenda,' in Alexander Gregor and Keith Wilson, *Postsecondary Education in Canada: The Cultural Agenda I* (Winnipeg: The University of Manitoba, 1986), pp. 1–23.

6 Surmounting the Insurmountable: Suggestions for Improving Canadian Public Education

A.E. Soles

For anyone who has spent a number of years either participating in, or observing the educational enterprise in Canada, it is not a feat of miraculous discernment or remarkable insight to identify a number of unresolved issues or problems which over time have continued to bedevil teachers, school administrators, school board members, government officials, parents and politicians. They are there. For the most part they are obvious, and they continue to cause controversy, debate and in some cases outright animosity!

These issues or problems appear to fall under two categories. First there are those which are obvious, are regularly debated and are really manifestations of large concerns. They include such matters as, student/teacher ratios, the status of the teaching profession, student evaluation, teacher evaluation, the curriculum, the teacher's role in school governance, the place of religion in the schools and so on. The second category includes those issues or problems which are much larger in scope, which appear to be endemic to Canadian education and are much more serious in terms of the future of the educational system. Included here would be such matters as public confidence in education, the funding of education, the growing support of private education and training, the purpose of education, leadership in education, and federal-provincial relations.

Let us begin with a brief examination of those issues which fall under the first category. First there is the matter of student/teacher ratio. It seems unlikely that teachers, parents or politicians will ever completely agree on what constitutes an optimum class size. The prolonged and dreary debate over student/teacher ratios will undoubtedly continue for some time to come. But if we cannot reach total agreement on what the optimum ratio should be, can we at least *approach* a consensus? Can we not reason together in a spirit of goodwill, and in an honest and unbiased attempt to do the best we can for education within the economic imperative imposed upon us by competing priorities in the social service sector? What does the best literature say about student/teacher ratios? Do such ratios apply equally in all disciplines? Have we tried hard enough to organize our classes or to set our timetables so that we might effectively operate with a mixture of large and small classes? Has any *serious* work really been done in timetable reorganization to accomplish such a mixture? Can the new teaching technologies help?

Surely we want for our children the best education possible, but let us acknowledge that society simply cannot afford the high salary costs that would inevitably follow the implementation of small classes in every discipline. Other sectors of society also make compelling demands — the poor, the sick, the elderly, the unemployed, the single parent. Our task is to find ways to provide quality education at a cost we can afford, while still allowing us to provide for other legitimate needs. Surely our aspirations are not so dissimilar, our beliefs so diverse, that no accommodation can be reached. But we must begin by talking together honestly — perhaps in small groups which may be less threatening, less given to rhetoric and less likely to lead to political posturing, than large groupings of representative factions. And let us begin by acknowledging that we share a problem in common.

Another area where debate and controversy will continue to abound, centres around the present status of the classroom teacher. Setting aside the rather unproductive debate as to whether teaching is a profession or a trade, we know that we can no longer ignore the fact that the teacher's prestige and the general esteem in which he or is she held by the public are at the lowest they have ever been. This statement may sound extreme, but it is not, I think, an exaggeration.

We might well wonder why a great and noble profession has fallen on such hard times. There are I suppose a number of reasons. In periods of severe financial restraint, when salaries are being cut or held at no increase, when job security is being threatened, when work loads are increasing under the guise of greater productivity, when a much higher level of accountability is being demanded both by government and the public in general, the profession not surprisingly, becomes both nervous and defensive. The voice of the militant trade unionist, always present but usually somewhat muted by the indifference of the majority of his or her colleagues, is now heard loudly as the body politic of the teaching profession attempts to get its message of concern across to taxpayers in general. But usually the voice is too strident, too militant, too threatening, the rhetoric too shrill, too angry and too political. The result is the alienation of the public who begin to see teachers as a group unwilling to share in bad times and interested only in themselves.

Such attitudes of course, play directly into the hands of certain politicians particularly those of right wing persuasion who continue to see all teachers as apologists of left wing ideologies and causes, and who, moreover believe them to be underworked and overpaid. Such sentiments are common within government officials both elected and appointed, and more significantly are shared by many individuals and groups in society as a whole. Such negative feelings deepen of course when teachers take action to try to express their concerns, because the only action open to them strikes directly, in one way or another, at the welfare of children. For the teacher, it is a no-win situation. And the result is that morale has never been lower.

'What is honoured in a country will be cultivated there'. Among other things, Plato was talking about education. Do we honour education? Have we cultivated it? The answer is clearly 'yes' to the extent that we have provided for its physical needs, by building and equipping fine schools, colleges and universities. But have we been concerned enough about those who teach in these edifices? Are we concerned about teacher morale, about the lack of prestige that most teachers now suffer? Are we concerned enough about the selection and training of teachers? We cannot honour education unless we honour those who teach. We need to begin *now* to create the kind of milieu, the kind of educational climate and context, where the high, crucial art of teaching can thrive again, and where the teacher can function not just as a knowledge technician but as a moulder of the generations to come. In my view, there is nothing more important today in moving towards consensus, than to restore the teaching profession to where it belongs as a great and noble calling.

Surely it is time that those who lead, be it in government, in industry or in education, recognize the teaching profession for what it is, a demanding calling and an essential service to all mankind, and in recognizing it, as such, begin to demonstrate and to articulate its importance. It is time to put an end to 'bad mouthing' teachers. It is time that teachers softened their rhetoric, recognized the harm they are doing to their profession, and set about improving their public image by the deeds they do.

It is in the best interest of society as a whole that whatever can be done ought to be done to restore the prestige of the classroom teacher and to reaffirm teaching as a great and noble profession. To this end it might well be time to consider the establishment under law of a College of Teachers, the responsibility of which would be to set standards of competency for entry and performance, generally to police the profession and rid it of undersirable elements, and finally to promote the general welfare and public relations for the profession as a whole. Insofar as possible, the College should limit its activities to purely professional concerns. It ought not to become yet another vehicle for bargaining salaries and/or working conditions. (Such a College has now been created in British Columbia.)

Another important area where consensus is lacking to the detriment of education generally is the whole matter of student evaluation. In British Columbia the situation is highlighted by the decision of the Ministry of Education to reinstate province-wide government examinations. This was a move resisted strongly by the teaching profession but supported generally by the public, who feel that a large majority of students graduating from our secondary schools are deficient in the skills and attitudes they will require to perform as successful individuals in an increasingly complex society.

But it seems to me that the debate as to whether examinations ought to be set and administered locally or provincially, obscures the real issue and begs the question as to the reliability and validity of the methods of evaluation presently in place in Canadian schools. To many thoughtful educators these methods seem strangely dated and appear to serve very little purpose in measuring what a student has learned from his school experience or in telling a prospective employer or an institution of higher learning what might be expected from someone who has been through the secondary school system.

But perhaps most significant of all is the implication left by the implementation of external examinations that teachers are not competent to evaluate their students. It is not surprising that teachers resent such an implication. When, however, they express their opposition (which may well be on legitimate educational grounds) they are accused of being afraid of having their teaching effectiveness examined by an independent examiner lest their incompetence or laziness or both should be revealed. It is clear that in many ways, teaching is a profession labouring under difficulties and to everyone's dissatisfaction.

The very important question of how we shall evaluate pupil progress or who should have the primary responsibility for carrying it out ought not to be so difficult a problem or so arcane an undertaking as to cause continuing debate and rancour. It is a matter which surely can and ought to be dealt with by the profession itself, including school administrators who appear to remain somewhat aloof from the whole matter. But it must be remembered that the evaluation of students is of major concern to a number of groups beyond the classroom and most of these are understandably intolerant of such notions that marks are unimportant or that competition is a bad thing which some educators have espoused. The public at large will continue to demand a certain standard of competence from those leaving school or university and they will expect competence to be measured and in terms they can understand. All who are directly involved in education, need to understand that while education has some responsibility to lead society and to break new ground, we must not forget that it is deeply imbedded in the life of the community and it reflects that life including its strengths and its weaknesses. Change occurs, but it occurs slowly and a good deal of patience and understanding is required on all sides.

The question of how well students have been taught, together with the related question of how well they know what they have been taught, which so often seems to exacerbate the lack of confidence of the school system as a whole, is all too frequently confused with *what* they have been taught. In short, much of the disagreement we encounter in this area may centre on the curricula itself. Here there would appear to be two continuing or recurring problems. What subjects, courses or programs should the curricula include, and what should the content of these courses or programs be?

In recent years, there appears to have been a tendency to add courses and programs to the curricula without concern for the amount of time being taken away from other subjects, many of which are basic to functional literacy. Such courses as local history, consumer education, and some others added either by Ministries of Education or by local authorities, detract from such crucial subjects as English, mathematics, science and social studies. Teachers cannot be expected to meet the expectations of prospective employers or institutions of higher learning if they are not given enough time to ensure mastery in core disciplines. Add to this the new area of study in computers and other disciplines needed by students in today's complex society, and we can begin to understand some of the difficult decisions educators now have to make. The content of the courses is also of prime importance. Is the course material up to date? Are the facts presented correctly? Is there redundancy? Are good, authoritative text books available? These, and a number of other questions must be addressed on a regular basis. Too often teachers are blamed for presenting material over which they have little control. Moreover, if they must gear their teaching to external examinations they will be quite reluctant to stray very far from the prescribed material.

But again, the questions of what should be taught, what subjects should be given special attention, what content ought to be included in the courses, what textbooks should be used, are surely not so complex as to defy solution. Surely some consensus is not beyond reach in this important area of education if the will to find common understanding and agreement is present.

The part that teachers might be allowed to play in the governance of education, particularly in the running of their schools, has become, in the last few years, another area of growing debate. Too often, unfortunately, the legitimate desires of teachers to play a more significant and professional role in the management of education generally and of the school in particular, have become encumbered by the perennial demands of the teacher unions for better working conditions, and conversely by school boards continuing to assert 'management rights'. In such a set of circumstances everyone loses. The teachers lose because they are denied the opportunity to become full participants in the educational enterprise and are expected to continue to function as quiet, obedient employees whose responsibilities are confined to a specific area. The school boards and their administrators also lose since they do not receive the valuable input from knowledgeable and concerned professionals, and much worse they lose their goodwill. And finally, the public in general, and the students in particular, lose as animosity deepens and teacher morale declines.

The irony in all of this is inescapable! Teachers attempts to become more involved in management continue to be rebuffed, while bureaucracy continues to flourish and to grow within the school itself, within the school board offices and within the ministries of education. It can be argued, of course, that the situation is not as bad as it might appear, since most of the bureaucrats are themselves trained teachers. We should not forget, however, how quickly these former teachers distance themselves, both physically and psychologically from the classroom.

The appropriate level of professional participation in institutional governance, will, it would appear, continue to be an abrasive and destructive issue. The bitter conflicts, more typical of industrial unions than of professional bodies are disruptive to the public school system and surely warrant new approaches to the status of the professional educator.

Again, the problem ought not to be insurmountable. Through sensitive and careful planning and discussion, it should be possible to establish the parameters whereby the traditional rights to manage by elected and appointed officials are not abrogated and where working conditions are changed *primarily* for the general improvement of learning, are affordable in cost, and will not be viewed solely as yet another point bargained for and won in a union contract.

There will, of course, always be difficulties in drawing the line between benefits to teachers and benefits to students. If student/teacher ratios, class sizes, the provision of specialists, the autonomy of the teacher in the classroom are really learning issues related specifically to the welfare of children, they should *never* be bargained against salary increases, sick leave provisions, group insurance or other matters traditionally fought for in industrial agreements. Moreover, if they *are* truly educational matters, they should never be subject to arbitration boards composed of members with no special understanding of the complications of the learning process.

In 1960, the Bureau of Educational Research at the University of Illinois published a document entitled *Government of Public Education for Adequate Policy Making*. In that publication, the distinguished educator Roald Campbell stated the view that it is essential for the public and professionals to interact 'in good faith' to both determine and implement basic educational goals successfully. If, however, we cannot achieve some agreement 'in good faith' it might be necessary to put in place a legislated process which would provide criteria for professional involvement in school district governance.

Teacher evaluation is also an area fraught with disagreement, frustration and general disillusionment. It is clear that the traditional methods of evaluation by Principals and school Superintendents have not gained much support from teachers, and indeed not much more from the school boards themselves. The reports written by school Principals and District Superintendents are typically not very informative documents. In the first place they are produced after a relatively short period of observation of the teacher's performance in the classroom. Secondly, because the observers (who also happen to be authority figures) are present in the classroom the situation tends to be both artificial and unnatural. The result is that most reports are generalized and jargon-laden, offering little by way of constructive criticism which might lead to overall improvement, and failing to be specific and frank about perceived weaknesses. As a matter of fact, as a result of a recent court case in British Columbia, where a teacher on the receipt of a negative report, sued her Principal and the Superintendent for libel and won, many school and school district administrators are afraid to be completely honest in what they write. Yet another factor militates against completely frank evaluations. When a negative report is written on a probationary teacher, the termination of his or her contract can be a fairly routine matter. However, in the case of a non-probationary teacher, the situation is very much different. Negative reports on teachers who have passed their probationary period, usually cause a clamour within the school board for their termination or transfer. Bringing such termination or transfer about is by no means a routine procedure but one which will involve the Principal and Superintendent in hours of discussion, meetings, public recriminations and the like. Most administrators simply don't want the drain on time and energy that such decisions cause. Hence they will tend to write a report so general and innocuous that no further action will be taken.

Admittedly, the whole matter of teacher evaluation is complex and difficult and the literature suggests that there are few if any jurisdictions where the processes in use or the policies in place to make good, evaluative judgements are considered satisfactory. And this despite the fact that in many of these jurisdictions the schemes are quite elaborate. While it seems unlikely that truly objective and informative evaluative techniques can ever be devised, one can only hope that the evaluation of teachers will always be given careful attention and that judgements, although subjective, when made by honest and experienced evaluators will improve the quality of classroom teaching. Judging the competence both in knowledge and in performance of any professional is of paramount interest to the public and particularly so in education where the majority of the 'clients' cannot make other choices.

The question of teacher competence inevitably brings us back to the teacher training institutions which now exist as Faculties of Education on university campuses. Like so many other aspects of education, the formal training of teachers is frequently under public and professional disapproval. Typically, Faculties of Education are accorded a low status in comparison with other professional schools or other programs offered on the campus. To some extent, the reason for this state of affairs is historical but one suspects that a good measure of academic snobbery enters the picture as well. At any rate the situation is unfortunate, because in many subtle but nevertheless tangible ways, the university says to the community at large and to its students in particular, that it does not give high priority to the development or the training of teachers. Again we are reminded of Plato's words; 'What is honoured in a country, will be cultivated there'. Given the undeniable fact that thoroughly trained and competent teachers are the cornerstone of the whole educational edifice, it seems little short of remarkable that teacher training is given so low a priority by the university personnel who train them and by the general population whose children are taught by them. We will have little chance of improving education until these attitudes which lead to short-sighted policies, can be changed.

Not all problems in education can be solved by the simple expedient of spending more money, but teacher training is one area that would benefit considerably from a healthy injection of funds. Most Faculties of Education are severely under-staffed given the important responsibilities they must assume over and above that of simply providing instruction. There is, for example, an important need for additional personnel to assist in screening the candidates who present themselves for admission. These personnel ought to be experienced educators, trained in interview techniques, and able to make informed judgements of the potential a candidate shows for becoming a good teacher or the aptitude he possesses for his calling. Another area where additional personnel are certainly required, is in supervision. Teacher trainees need to spend more time in real classrooms under the close supervision of well experienced instructors who not only can give them invaluable assistance, but can also make the best judgements on their suitability for the teaching profession.

The training of our future teachers and the upgrading of our present ones is surely a matter of some importance and deserving of a much greater investment of time, energy and money than has been the case in the past. We ought, for example, to implement some internship programs (perhaps of varying lengths) at least on a pilot basis. Under such a scheme, the subsidization of trainees, the need for increased supervision or release time within the selected schools would all have to be taken into account and would no doubt be expensive. But if significant improvement in the quality of teachers produced could be demonstrated, the money would be well spent. We need also, attractive scholarship schemes to encourage our best undergraduates to consider a career in education. In this connection, it is worth noting that many more able students would consider entering teaching if they believed the training programs to be more rigorous and the competition to enter more intense. Too often, because of the attitude of the university community generally, and the experience of graduates of some teacher training programs, education is thought to be a 'mickey-mouse' discipline for second-rate scholars. Given its supreme importance to the development of a sound educational system, the training and upgrading of teachers must no longer be neglected. Today it remains as one of the most important unresolved issues in education.

A final issue that from time to time surfaces in Canadian education is the place of religion in the schools. In an increasingly pluralistic society it is not surprising that this should become a major unresolved issue. Whether the 'Lord's Prayer' should be said in our classrooms, or the Bible read, is a decision which must ultimately be made by the state. There would appear however, to be little purpose in insisting upon a practice that many teachers refuse, on the grounds of conscience, to carry out. It is doubtful in fact that under the constitution they can be required to do so.

Whether or not a given creed should be continued or introduced, the whole important question of values in education is still one which deserves attention and is largely forgotten in the debate over the place of religion in state schools. Again this is an area of considerable complexity, but it ought not to be too difficult to see that certain values or habits of behaviour should be inculcated in our youth. Surely such values as racial and religious tolerance, a sense of justice, an attitude of caring and compassion for those less fortunate than ourselves, courtesy, and the like are worth teaching to our students either directly, or perhaps, more effectively through the judicious selection of learning materials related to such disciplines as literature, social studies, art and the sciences. Everything, of course, will depend upon the value placed on the teaching of such attitudes or behaviour by the teachers themselves. At any rate, whether or not more emphasis should be placed on the inculcation of such values is yet another unresolved issue in Canadian education.

The issues which we have discussed to this point are those which most obviously cause tension and dissent among teachers, school boards, parents, government officials and the public generally. We should not of course forget the value that a certain degree of tension or even controversy brings to our lives and to the institutions we have created. Whether to perform great deeds of daring or write great poems, compose great music, or even to fly a kite (which in itself is a kind of metaphor on life) some kind of tension must be present. When our sociologists talk about 'creative tension' I presume they mean a condition or a state of mind that allows us to move forward out of our complacency or out of our ignorance to purposeful action and to meaningful learning. It should not surprise us therefore, that tension should exist in education. It is, indeed, axiomatic that learning cannot take place without it.

It is well to remember, however, that education does not take place only within the confines of a classroom where tension, controversy and debate can be channelled by a skilful teacher into a productive learning activity. Nor does learning take place only between a pupil and a teacher. Education is, as we all know, a particularly human enterprise involving an extraordinary number of varied and complex relationships — student to teacher, student to parent, teacher to parent, teacher to school board, school board to parent, school board to government and so on. To a greater or lesser degree, each of these groups will hold different values, have different expectations, dream different dreams. This condition is particularly manifest today. One of the constants of contemporary society is diversity — diversity of creed, of culture, of race, of custom. Of course, such diversity has always been present, but before the explosive developments in transportation and communication transformed the world into a global village, the differences were largely hidden in separate enclaves. No longer so! Gone are those times when a certain unity of belief, a tacit agreement on values, a similarity of custom, were predominant in Canadian society and hence in Canadian classrooms where that society is reflected. Gone are that days when ways were known and understood. Today we live with differences and whereas tension and controversy have always existed, they are now likely to be more pronounced and more articulate than ever before. All too frequently, (and sadly), they have become a destructive rather than a creative element in Canadian education.

Any hope that we might somehow build a consensus among these many different groups who participate in the education enterprise, or that we might somehow be able to restore a climate of cooperation and good will, must take into account that controversy, debate and tension among those various groups will continue to exist and may indeed increase. The task before us is to find a way to channel the tension along creative paths and to learn from our differences. We simply have to find a way to reason together in a climate that is free of mistrust and hostility.

To this end, we might, as a first step, begin with very small and informal groups of people with differing views but who are genuinely trying to reach some common ground — the reverse of a 'summit meeting'. Having established a number of such cells, we might at the outset limit our discussion to several broad but central issues which must first be addressed before tackling the more specific ones we have been discussing. There are a number of these broad concerns. Let us examine some of the obvious ones.

The time has come to acknowledge that the so-called professionals in education together with the lay people with active interest, for example board members, have done an extremely poor job of building confidence in public education. And we should not forget to include government officials and politicians. We have quarreled among ourselves publicly to the point that we have utterly confused and angered the people who have to pay the tax bill. Remarkably, these citizens have continued to be patient throughout all of this debate and to show a willingness to pay the high costs of education. But unless they can see some agreement or harmony among those who are perceived as experts, they are likely to become increasingly impatient and indifferent.

How public education can be 'sold' (in the good sense of that term) to the public generally, is in itself a major unresolved issue in education, and all levels and kinds of publicly supported education are implicated since the public tends to see all parts as interrelated.

The funding of education at all levels continues to be of major concern and this is a concern which will deepen in direct proportion to the loss of public confidence. Politicians have already read public opinion well and are convinced that education is not a 'political winner' as it may have been in the 1960s. It is well to keep in mind that politicians run on the fuel of public opinion. Education will receive the support that the public demands for it — witness recent developments in California and the Irish Republic. It is surely time that our own educators, both lay and professional got their acts together and stopped alienating Canadian taxpayers. It is time also that our own federal and provincial governments came to grips with the issue of support for education and training. To fail to do so is to place our country at a most serious disadvantage with other western industrial nations.

Today there appears to be developing a trend toward the public support of private education and training. In some ways this seems to be a desperation move on the part of governments who know that they must do something and yet have a sense that public education is failing society. They simply don't know where else to turn. Clearly they are not getting very helpful answers from the educational community itself, only (as the MacDonald Royal Commission rather acidly points out) requests for more money! But apart from the tedious arguments, and at times, petty quarrels which in the last few years have all too frequently surrounded and demeaned education, we might wonder whether there are not deeper reasons for the loss of confidence being expressed in so many quarters.

We might begin by asking ourselves what as educators we are trying to achieve. Most of us can agree that the main purpose of education is to equip people with the attitudes, information, and skills required to perform as successful individuals in a increasingly complex human society.

History teaches us that there is a wide range of attitudes towards almost every aspect of human behaviour and human interaction with the physical and biological worlds. Moreover, the body of human knowledge of the world and indeed of themselves, is being added to constantly. The facts of any one time are constantly subject to re-definition in light of new information. As Robert Oppenheimer once remarked 'the world alters as we walk in it'. The skills which are needed or desired at any one time are likely to alter steadily or sporadically throughout life.

The evidence we have before us so far, seems to suggest that the formal education of the young, should concentrate upon equipping them with the basis for reasoning, the requirements of learning, the capacity to adapt and an appreciation of intellectual rigour and of excellence in performance. Over and above these will come the training required to equip them to perform useful roles in some field of endeavour. Unfortunately, it seems all too clear, even to the most sympathetic observer, that the large majority of our students graduating from high school today, are deficient in these requirements. This general deficiency exists as a major indictment of our system of public education and must be regarded as the single most important issue facing it today.

How can the problem be corrected? Undoubtedly the solution lies in a major restructuring of the educational imperative which will require the addition of some new disciplines, the deletion of some others and a new emphasis on some existing ones. A partial and perhaps too simplistic a list of these requirements might include;

(a)   A thorough familiarity with the language of the society (either English or French) including a greater emphasis than before upon the anatomy of the language acquired through linguistics or grammar. An ability to use words precisely is an obvious need.

(b)   Since much decision making now depends upon electronically processed data, an understanding of computer processing, the basis for numerical reasoning and a fundamental knowledge of statistics are essential.

(c)   Numeracy. Today it seems that a grasp of mathematical logic is even more essential than before, plus some experience in mathematical reasoning through the study of algebra or analytical geometry.

(d)   History. Students ought to be taught the historical method of thought, reasoning and evidence. They should be introduced to the major evolutionary trends of thought among different peoples and in different times.

(e)   Students need to be given a much better understanding of social and physical geography than they now have.

(f)   Students need an understanding of behavioural science and social biology and ecology. The survival of our planet may well depend upon this knowledge.

(g)   Students should have some knowledge of the evolution of the Fine Arts and their place in society.

(h)   Students should have some basic knowledge of economics, government and law.

There will, of course, always be a temptation to add subjects to a curriculum, and it is imperative that we be selective if we hope to achieve some mastery of the subjects taught. We must strive to reach some common agreement on what it is we want our students to learn and having reached that agreement set about to provide the best course content, the best learning materials, the best text books and the best trained teachers we can find. Only in this way can we begin to restore some confidence in our educational system.

But all this means that we must have a clear vision of the kind of world we live in today, are likely to live in tomorrow and of what is essential for young people to know in order to live useful rewarding and productive lives. Not everyone can be blessed with such vision. It is, in truth a gift or an ability, reserved for a few and it is an essential part of good leadership.

Clearly the question of leadership in education, or perhaps the lack of it, is a major issue which needs to be addressed. In doing so we need to make clear at once that there is an important difference between good management and good leadership. They are not the same thing. As Dressel points out in his book *Administrative Leadership* (1981), leadership is knowing where to go whereas management is knowing how to get there. Defining precisely what leadership is, however, is not easy. The problem seems to be that most definitions focus on a leader's characteristics, not on what leaders do. Michael Maccoby, in *The Leader* (1981), reminds us that leaders are usually intelligent, hard working, competitive, caring, flexible, trustworthy and so on but many persons who share these characteristics are not leaders. Focusing on characteristics has not been very helpful. Richard Cyert, President of Carnegie Mellon University and organizational behaviourist, states that leadership is 'the ability to bring about conformity between sub-group goals and total organizational goals'. As somewhat similar explanation is given by Gardner: 'Leadership... is the process of persuasion by which an individual induces a group to take action that is in accord with the leader's purposes or the shared purposes of all.'[2] These definitions take us beyond personal characteristics towards general kinds of performance.

We do know that leaders exercise influence well beyond that defined by their authority or formal position alone. There are Principals and principals, Superintendents and superintendents. The differences in their organizational performances are largely the differences in their leadership abilities.

In a paper presented to the 1986 Annual Meeting of the Canadian Association for Continuing Education, Jack P. Blaney, the Vice-President of University Development at Simon Fraser University, listed seven things that leaders as distinct from managers do. He compiled this list having made a content analysis of thirteen books dealing with the subject of leadership and considered by reviewers to be commendable additions to the literature on the subject. As elicited from the thirteen examined books, the corporate elite do several mutually reinforcing things that others do not do;

(a) Leaders create and articulate a vision for their organization.
(b) Leaders combine their vision with a few, fundamental values concerning what is important to the organization and how it should work.
(c) Leaders obsessively centralize vision and values, but then decentralize everything else, empowering their associates to work with energy and imagination.
(d) Leaders institutionalize innovation and entrepreneurship.
(e) Leaders persist in marketing their organization.
(f) Leaders simplify.
(g) And finally, leaders throughout their organization, but also well beyond their organization, establish trust.

And Blaney concludes, 'Leaders are persistent and they persist in doing these things. In doing so, they energize themselves and others towards the achievement of important objectives.'[3]

To the dispassionate observer, there seems little evidence that leadership of the quality suggested above, exists in any great measure in our school systems or in most ministries of education. Good management practised by well-trained managers, is often present, but not good leadership. It may well be that the bureaucratic nature of the educational system militates against the development of those qualities of mind and spirit which great leaders possess, or at least makes it difficult for them to put into practice the imaginative and innovative ideas they develop. The nature of bureaucracy is to make the organization tidy and to keep it free of risk. In such an environment, change comes slowly and innovation and imagination are not normally encouraged.

Yet another area where unresolved issues remain, concerns the extent to which the fierce defence of provincial autonomy in education affects the development of appropriate national objectives. While the debate is presently focused most sharply at the post-secondary level, it now begins to cut across all educational boundaries, because of the growing impact of technology on our society.

It seems clear that the most significant result of advancing technology has been the growing technological inter-dependence of communities and provinces throughout Canada and throughout the diverse jurisdictions within the international community. Imparting the ability to understand and participate in global technological and social change, is essential to secure the enfranchisment of all people in an environment in which advancing technology can become a tool in the concentration of power.

The *O.E.C.D. Review of National Policies in Education: Canada* published in 1976 referred to the strong political and cultural implications of Canada's regional differences while deploring the lack of national policies of education. This lack of clearly stated national policies for education at the public school level has resulted in inadequate articulation between and among provinces so that students moving from one provincial jurisdiction to another often experience placement difficulties. Corporate people have, for many years expressed concern over the situation. It seems that the transfer of employees between provinces is increasing. People with families are more likely to be moving across the country to match their skills with available employment. There seems to be a clear indication that we should attempt some standardization of curriculum across the country. That a student should suffer placement difficulties in transferring from one province to another is unacceptable.

The Council of Ministers of Education, Canada (CMEC) has attempted over the years to address the question of standardizing the curriculum, and other national educational concerns but with little success. Transcending the regional and cultural differences that characterize this nation will never be easy as the CMEC well knows. It has found it extremely difficult to reach a Canadian consensus on even relatively minor educational matters. It is one of the continuing but sad ironies for those who have been active over the years in the Council of Ministers that the only time the Council can truly reach consensus is when it is attacking a policy or a program being advanced by the federal government.

While we can argue with some validity that much of our strength as a nation lies in our diversity, we should also understand that the foundation of our national identity and indeed of our democratic society, will ultimately be based on the common, shared experience of our public school system. Surely it is important to the future of our people, that we give a high priority to its care and cultivation.

Notes

1 Richard M. Cyert, 'Academic Leadership' *Continuum*, vol. 49 no. 2 (Spring 1985), p. 124.

2 John W. Gardner, 'The Nature of Leadership' *Leadership Papers/1* (Washington, D.C.: Independent Sector, 1986), p. 6.

3 Jack P. Blaney, 'Leaders in University Continuing Education: Challenges, Opportunities and Tasks,' a paper presented to the Canadian Association for Continuing Education, 1986, manuscript.

7 Quality in Canadian Public Education: Some Future Perspectives

Norman Henchey

There are many perspectives from which to choose for a critical assessment of Canadian education, but these perspectives can be situated along two axes, one for indicators of educational quality and the other for time.

There are six major indicators of educational quality;

- (a) Assumptions and expectations as the justification for policy and practice;
- (b) Clientele satisfaction, the reaction of students, parents, or employers;
- (c) Coherence and suitability of structures, effectiveness, articulation among levels, fairness;
- (d) Resource efficiency in terms of money and use of personnel;
- (e) Relevance for social, political and economic context;
- (f) Effectiveness of results as measured by examinations and subsequent performance of the graduates of the system.

Each of these indicators provides us with a different kind of evaluation and a different method of arriving at this evaluation. The quality of a system's expectations may be high but the structures may be unsuitable and the results poor. Clientele may be satisfied but the system may be inefficient in the use of resources and not tuned to the economic structure of the society.

The second axis is in reference to time: (a) Continuity with the past; (b) Reflection of the present; (c) Preparation for the future. Of course, every education system is a mix of all three time perspectives. It has a history and tradition upon which it is based and which it is mandated to reproduce, in some edited version, for a new generation; it is a mirror of the present, reflecting changing realities, often slowly and with difficulty; it is a projection of images of the future, of trends, possibilities, needs, and hopes. When the social rhythm follows an easy and measured flow from past to present to future, an education system has a clear mandate and its quality is easily judged; it prepares for the future through the past and the present.

When there is turbulence and discontinuity, the past may be an unreliable, even dangerous, guide, and the present may be unstable and difficult to read. At such a time, the perspective of the future is at once blurred and crucial as an approach to the quality of education, a screen difficult to read but one on which we may write.

The issue of the quality of Canadian public education is approached in this paper from the double perspective of context and future, of Canadian society and where we may be going as Canadians during the years that remain in this century and millennium. To do this, there are seven questions that we should consider:

- (a) What is a future perspective?
- (b) What are the major social functions of the education system today?
- (c) On what assumptions is the present education system based?
- (d) What are the major social trends that are shaping Canada's present and future?
- (e) What challenges are these trends presenting to the education system?
- (f) How could public education meet these challenges?
- (g) To what extent is public education preparing for the future?

A Future Perspective

The study of the future arises out of our need to anticipate the consequences of trends and actions (what is often called foresight) and our desire to have a hand in creating and shaping our individual and collective destiny. From our need to anticipate come projections of *probable* futures and explorations of *possible* futures, alternatives to those being shaped by current trends. From our wish to create the future come the elaboration of *preferable* futures based on values and assumptions and the design of *plausible* futures that seem within our capacity to establish and manage. Thus futurists are not people who predict but rather those who project what is likely, propose what is desirable and possible, and warn against what is probable and undesirable.

Since the Second World War, the study of the future has developed as a field of research and as a profession. It has become institutionalized in associations, conferences, journals, institutes and projects, and it has been popularized through the work of Herman Kahn, Alvin Toffler, John Naisbitt, the Club of Rome, the World Future Society, and UNESCO. Canada, too, has discovered the future with institutes such as GAMMA in Montreal, associations such as the Canadian Association for Future Studies, and Government interest shown in work of the Science Council of Canada and the 'Canada Tomorrow' Conference held in 1983.

In general, studies of the future include an identification and analysis of major recent and current trends, the extrapolation of these trends, the development of alternative scenarios, the exploration of values and choices, and the design of policies and strategies which may lead to the reduction or solution of problems. In recent years, the major preoccupations of futurists have been the protection of the environment, the social impact of technology, disparity in wealth and power among nations and groups, alternatives to war as a means of resolving conflict, the protection of human rights, and the improvement of major political, social, economic and educational institutions.

A future perspective, then, is one that looks at the present from the other side of history, not from the origins and causes of present events but from their consequences and implications.

The Social Functions of Education

In Canada, as in most countries, public education is a complex social enterprise. While we are often inclined to take its assumptions, structures and institutions for granted as natural and necessary elements of social progress, what we call public education is a relatively recent phenomenon in history, developed in Europe and North America mainly during the past century. This history of public education explains its functions and characteristics.

Public education has three major functions: moral, economic and intellectual. The moral functions include socializing young people in the customs and *mores* of the society, sorting pupils into different categories for further schooling and work, controlling them through various disciplinary rules, and providing custodial care during their period of dependency, keeping them off the streets when they are young and off the labour market when they are older. The economic functions of schools tie them to the labour market as the producers of manpower (or human resources as we now prefer to think of them), the basis of society's economic investment in education; there is also a consumption aspect of learning, activities which lead more to personal enjoyment and development than to direct economic benefit. The intellectual functions of schools involve training in skills, especially those of communication, imparting information, and stimulating critical and creative thinking.

While educators like to stress the intellectual functions of schooling and certain aspects of the moral function such as the inculcating of good habits, it is the sorting, custodial and productive functions of public education that are often the *de facto* priorities of planners, government leaders, employers and university registrars. Thus, from the perspective of the social context, the quality of Canada's schools weighs more on the scales of the identification of talent, success in instilling key social values such as respect and responsibility, the ability of graduates to enter smoothly into the job market than it does on the scales of critical inquiry, common wisdom or personal well-being. Nor is it impossible to imagine circumstances in which certain social functions (good citizenship) may militate against other functions (critical thinking).

The Assumptions of the Public School

Because public schools developed in a particular period of time and in particular places, they acquired a character that reflected western industrial society. First, schools were based on the assumption that knowledge was scarce and that schools had a monopoly on it. Though there were always educated but unschooled people, as school systems evolved they acquired more and more control over the definition and recognition of what constituted important knowledge (what was on the curriculum). For most people, schools were islands of knowledge and virtue in a sea of ignorance and sin.

Second, as a logical and legal extension of the monopoly of schools, schooling became compulsory, the normal avenue to adulthood. Schools were a protection for children against abuse and ignorance, and so the state assumed greater and greater control over the education of the young, providing resources, certifying teachers, approving curriculum and attesting to the competence of those who left as graduates and the lack of competence of those who 'dropped out'.

Third, schools developed a core curriculum that was derived from their three functions. Schools furthered their social functions of sorting, socializing and controlling children through the hidden curriculum of rituals, rules and relationships and the use of certain subjects (Latin, mathematics, French immersion) as sorting mechanisms. The economic functions of schools were furthered through formal programs of vocational training (technical and business courses), through pre-university programs in language, mathematics and science, as well as through a hidden curriculum promoting punctuality, sense of responsibility, efficiency and self-discipline. The intellectual functions were promoted by historical conceptions of disciplines as bodies of knowledge, some more important than others.

Fourth, schools came to be modelled on industrial structures, especially in North America, adopting the powerful and successful metaphor of industry in their curriculum as the course to be run, in competition, schedules, courses, group instruction, specialization, testing, marks, certification and in the bureaucracy of structures and roles.

Finally, schools were based on the separation of work as job, education as schooling, and leisure as entertainment. School was the transition between play (the unreal world) and work (the real world) and it was a preparation for life.'

Major Social Trends

Canadian education has generally reflected the structure and served the needs of a society whose economy was based on natural resources and manufacturing, whose standard of living, culture and life-style reflected in many ways those of the United States, and whose traditions and values were conservative and cautious. Yet in the past decade Canadian society has been changing dramatically as the result of the impact of five major trends: (a) the changing place of knowledge in society, (b) the revolution in communications technology, (c) the converging patterns of work, learning, and leisure, (d) growing complexity and turbulence, and (e) increasing pluralism.

Canada is rapidly being transformed into an information economy and a *knowledge society*. The quantity of information is increasing exponentially; methods of acquiring, verifying, managing and disseminating information, especially through computers, are becoming more powerful and accessible; new theories of knowledge, new systems of organizing knowledge, and new paradigms are challenging traditional assumptions of the nature and limits of human rationality; developments in brain research on the one hand and in artificial intelligence on the other are expanding our understanding of the nature of learning; the applications of knowledge, the links between research and development, and the evolution of the 'knowledge industries' are changing the place of knowledge in the economy. We are now living in a society in which knowledge, more than land, money and labour, is the major source of wealth, employment and power.

Parallel to the transformation of knowledge in our society is a revolution in *communications technology*. While the most visible elements of this technology are the hardware of computers, satellites, VCRs, laser disks, optical fibres and chips, the revolution in communications is creating an integrated technological system, an electronic culture and an artificial reality. This system is rapidly being applied to manufacturing through robots, to banking, record keeping, security, office practice, mail, publishing and professional expertise in medicine, law, and engineering. This technology raises important questions about the meaning of human intelligence in a world of artificial intelligence, the value of human work in a world of robots, the right to privacy in a interconnected system of data bases, the concepts of knowledge and ignorance in a world of information overload, and the meaning of sanity in an environment of 'artificial reality.'

The patterns of *work, learning and leisure* are changing, partly as the result of the combined effects of knowledge and communications and partly because of social change, diversity of values, and shifting demographic patterns in Canadian society. The traditional sequence of early childhood (leisure), later childhood and adolescence (learning), adulthood (work) and old age (leisure) is breaking down. We now find the period of formal learning extending downward towards infancy and upward to post-secondary studies and adult education. At the other end, older Canadians are retiring younger, living longer and better, and becoming more demanding in their expectations for quality leisure, meaningful work and stimulating learning. In the middle, between learning and leisure, the period of work is becoming shorter, the work week is reduced, holidays are longer; technology is removing many jobs and more women are competing for those jobs that do exist; part-time employment, underemployment, unemployment and periods between employment are becoming 'normal'; jobs are becoming polarized between the relatively few that are high-skilled and the many that are low-skilled. Work is becoming a scarce commodity; jobs are changing and people are changing their jobs. A substantial part of many jobs is devoted to learning, many leisure activities are really work, more and more learning occurs not in youth and not in schools, but throughout life and in a variety of settings. The period of compulsory schooling is becoming a smaller and smaller element in the ongoing process of lifelong learning.

Life in contemporary Canada is increasingly *complex*. We are living in an age of change and turbulence in our economic structures, social institutions, and political activity. Conventional wisdom, traditional ethnic and religious affiliations and other sources of identity and meaning are losing their hold on our confidence and their power to explain events and guide us. The solution to one problem often contains the seeds of an even more serious and complex one. Leaders find their range of options limited, their trade-offs more problematic, their public support fragile and uncertain. Many people are adrift, while many others, faced with this complexity, turn to the security offered by the past, by cults, by fundamentalist religious groups, or by cultural or political stereotypes, all promising easy, simple and unequivocal answers to difficult, complex and ambiguous questions.

The fifth major trend is the multi-dimensional *pluralism* in Canadian society. We have tended to think of pluralism in Canada largely in terms of ethnicity, religion, and language and we have not always succeeded in dealing with this pluralism in a sensitive way. Now, in addition to many religions, languages and ethnic groups, we have pluralism in the cultures of different age groups, of the sexes, of professional and social-class affiliations, lifestyle patterns, family structures, and regional identities. These intersecting pluralities, reinforced by a general spirit of individualism and a structure of personal and group rights and entitlements, are pressing institutions with often exaggerated expectations and often conflicting demands.

These five broad trends in Canadian society (knowledge, communications, work-learning-leisure patterns, complexity and pluralism) are powerful forces which individually, and in their combined impact, are transforming Canada. They are challenging our assumptions; they are causing us to question the value of our existing institutions; they are forcing us to adjust our way of life, careers, and expectations; they are testing our ability to deal with uncertainty, to cope with ambiguity; they are rushing Canada into a global village of competition, conflict, and interdependence. The Canada of the 1990s will not be able to rely on its Mounties, wheat, hydroelectric power, lumber, sub-contracts, royal commissions and the C.B.C. to maintain the quality of living to which we have become accustomed.

Challenge to Education

These five trends shaping the present and the future can be seen as both a challenge to public education and the criteria by which its quality may be judged. The transformation of knowledge and its growing importance in our society challenge the curriculum of elementary and secondary education and forces us to re-think the criteria by which content should be selected. The new communications technologies challenge existing systems of access to learning and they suggest new ways to conceive of a learning system, new definitions of 'literacy,' and new methods for making learning more effective. Changing patterns of work, learning and leisure challenge existing structures of formal and compulsory education, and the relation between formal and non-formal institutions, and they make the concept of continuing or lifelong education the perspective from which to judge public schooling. Complexity is a challenge to goals and priorities and forces us to consider the degree to which public education exposes learners to different value and meaning systems. Pluralism is a challenge to our institutions to adapt to diverse needs and expectations and to be judged by the extent to which they are responsive to both the common good of the society and the particular rights of individuals and groups within it. We can summarize the trends, challenges and criteria in this way:

Trends	Challenges	Criteria
Knowledge	curriculum	selection of content
Communications	system	access, literacy, effectiveness
Work-Learning-Leisure	formal structure	continuing, lifelong education
Complexity	priorities	meaning and value systems
Pluralism	institutions	adaptation and responsiveness

In recent years, many countries have launched a re-examination of their core curricula, especially at the secondary level. They are questioning the substance, relevance, rigour and effectiveness of curriculum and are considering various proposals touching on the selection of content, its sequence and structure, and the levels of expectation for learning. A number of international conferences have been held on the subject of core curriculum and the content of general education.

The transformation of knowledge poses two major challenges to curriculum policy. First, what knowledge, skills, and values should be selected as the core curriculum for all learners in public education? Second, how does the changing role of knowledge in the society and the economy affect the role of schools to prepare young people for citizenship and employment? The first challenge is one of general and academic education and the meaning of the educated person in the last decade of the 20th century; the second challenge is one of social and vocational education and the preparation of people to live and work in the information society which Canada is becoming.

The challenge of knowledge is far more complex and profound than asking how much mathematics or language or social sciences should be taught. It asks: what mathematics? What topics should be priorities? How can technological aids such as computers and pocket calculators reduce the priority and time given to certain topics? What is the amount of time that should be devoted to mathematics in relation to other areas such as the arts, language, science, fitness, personal development, history and all the other areas that may make a claim for inclusion in core programs? How much attention in history and geography should be devoted to the study of Canada, to our western tradition, to non-western cultures, to the Middle Ages, to the contemporary Middle East? There is no limit to the number of topics that can be included in the curriculum of any area of knowledge and no limit to the number of areas of knowledge that can make a legitimate claim for a place in the curriculum. The task is to determine the priorities, to decide what purposes must take precedence, and to seek ways of making these decisions.

The new communications technology challenges our concept of an education system built on formal institutions, group instruction, fixed time, and physical presence in a specific location. A technology that is now transforming many areas of work, many professions, and much of our cultural life has hardly begun to intrude on our systems of learning. Computers are being domesticated and incorporated into computer labs, hardly challenging the existing structures and operations of schools; they are seen as a supplement to group instruction, having little effect on how and when we learn, only marginally used to extend access to learning to new clientele, not challenging the assumptions of existing systems. We are only beginning to incorporate communications technology in our repertoire of the learning skills essential for all students: use of databases, computer-based catalogues, word-processing, media literacy (both creative and critical use of communications technology), and software programs to enhance our learning of concepts and skills. The new technologies offer a new system of access to learning that can transform our existing learning systems, expand our potential to reach learners, and create new ways of learning 'how to learn'.

As we no longer divide our lives neatly into compartments of leisure, learning and work, our general structure of formal and non-formal learning must be reconsidered to meet changing needs, a broader range of possibilities, and more diverse clientele. Since the early 1970s, continuing education has been regularly promoted as a philosophical and organizational framework within which all learning activities could be situated: formal and non-formal structures, young and adult clients, general and specialized studies, traditional and innovative methods, academic and practical forms of learning.

Until now, however, continuing education has been largely relegated to the groves of rhetoric and to the field of adult education, a matter of pious exhortation or a service added to existing structures and budgets, important mainly in periods of high unemployment and declining public school enrolments. Yet a broad policy of continuing education, if taken seriously, would challenge public education in three ways: first, by situating elementary, secondary and post-secondary education as the initial phase of the learning services offered to persons, to be supplemented by other resources and services; second, the human and financial resources which the society commits to learning would shift from one priority to another depending on need; and third, formal education would be integrated more closely with non-formal learning activities in the media, voluntary sector, business, community development, the activities of professions, and cultural institutions. Public education in such an integrated policy may be of less importance than it now is in the overall repertoire of learning resources and the broader learning agenda.

The increasing complexity of our lives and of the issues with which we must deal challenges the education system to establish its priorities; it challenges schools to provide learners with ways of constructing meaning systems and structures of values. There are many social indicators which underline the importance of meaning and value systems, especially for young people: suicide rate, mindless violence, drug and alcohol abuse, casual or exploitive sex, apathy, alienation, loneliness, and lack of purpose. The youth culture of 'Walkmans', rock videos, heavy metal and 'Pac-man' needs some supplement of history, cultural choices and alternative values. Preserving some balance in an era of often frantic change, maintaining calm in the face of uncertainty and ambiguity, and being patient in the pursuit of solutions to complex and difficult problems are all matters that must preoccupy public education.

Some major issues deserve both intellectual and moral attention in public education: the meaning of being a person in an advanced technological society, the rights of women, the place of minorities in the majority culture, the interaction of cultural communities, ways of dealing with violence, the protection of the environment, the place of Canada in North American and world affairs, ethical questions raised by new medical and biological technologies, imbalances in the distribution of wealth and power, the excesses of the consumer society, and many more. An education can be judged by the quality and substance of the issues which it presents to learners and by the stimulation and support it offers them in their encounter with these issues.

Schools and school systems are already struggling with the challenges of pluralism. The ethnic and social consensus on which they traditionally relied is now being replaced by diversity in traditions, beliefs, priorities, expectations and values. Schools, especially those in urban centres, can no longer expect their students to adjust to traditional expectations of French, English, male, female, white, middle-class cultural norms. To a greater or lesser extent, every Canadian school is multicultural; if students must adapt to schools, the culture of schools must also adapt to the students and the communities of which they are a part. It is not easy for schools which are part of complex bureaucratic structures to shift from the managerial neatness of uniformity to the uncertainty and complexity of adaptation and diversity.

Many schools must deal with the reality that the culture and language of instruction are the first culture and language of only a minority of their clients; many Catholic schools must deal with a pluralism of belief among their teachers as well as among their pupils and parents; competition, punctuality, assertiveness, disciplined work habits and a sustained interest in abstract tasks are values more prized in some cultures than in others. Many teachers find themselves trying to reach across cultural chasms; many cultural signs and symbols are misread. Deep in the mythology of the public school is the value of shared vision, equality of opportunity, and common services, the ideal that individual and group characteristics and priorities can be accommodated within the framework of a common school structure, a proving ground for the accommodations needed in the larger society. Important segments of our society opt out of this mythology in favour of the more particularistic cultures of private schools, religious schools, or alternative schools, institutions in which they find a sharper focus and more congenial environment than they see in the public school system. These groups outside the public school, no less than those within, challenge the capacity of public education to adapt to pluralism in a responsive and creative way.

Meeting the Challenge

There is little doubt that learning must be a central project of the emerging knowledge society in Canada; there may be more doubt, however, about whether the existing structures and institutions of public elementary and secondary education will rise to meet these challenges or whether they will become marginalized as other structures and institutions assume greater responsibility for learning. Scriptoria did not meet the challenges of movable type and it remains to be seen whether schools will be the scriptoria of the 21st century.

If public education in Canada is to engage the trends shaping the larger society, it must re-think its existing policies and move in new directions. To deal with the changing place of knowledge, it must evaluate and monitor in an on-going way, the content of elementary and secondary education, setting priorities, eliminating repetition, pruning low-priority topics, identifying content priorities. There needs to be continuing and substantial public and professional debate on the content of general education; educational leaders must take the moral responsibility of demonstrating that, backed by compulsory attendance laws, they are not permitting young people to pass their time on the curricular equivalent of 'Trivial Pursuit'.

We have a rich cultural and intellectual heritage upon which to draw for our curriculum and an active scholarly and moral community (in universities, research institutes, religious, cultural and voluntary organizations, government and the private sector) upon which to rely for developing, pruning, organizing, and evaluating elementary and secondary school curriculum. Curriculum development involves the identification of key concepts that must be stressed in learning programs: limits, trade-offs, symbols, systems, conservation, interdependence, change, learning, authority, equity, and diversity, as a beginning. Parallel to these are key skills of dealing with reality: anticipation of consequences, effective participation in group action, use of information systems, communicating in a variety of media, creative problem solving, conflict mediation, and logic. Fundamental values include tolerance for ambiguity, appreciation of diversity, responsibility, pride in the quality of our work, sense of confidence, compassion.

To meet the communications revolution, three steps would have to be taken. First, we must change our image of the integration of 'education technology' into existing structures and procedures to one of integrating existing structures and procedures into an emerging learning network, including schools, television, VCRs, computers, electronic mail, satellites, and computer-aided learning. Second, we must recognize that the new technologies require new basic learning skills if they are to be used effectively and critically, especially the ability to learn and communicate by a variety of media, reducing and organizing information, using word-processing and data bases, and seeing in the new technology its potential for enriching our lives and enlarging our vision. Third, we must re-think our concept of teaching methods, our systems of access to learning, our notion of attendance, and the function of teaching. The major pedagogical challenge in the coming years is to develop principles for determining the right 'mix' of technology, persons, resources, and institutions which would be appropriate for different learning objectives and different learning clienteles. Mastery of inferential statistics for senior secondary students may be mainly a matter of appropriate computer software; helping emotionally vulnerable children to enjoy poetry may be largely a combination of a sensitive teacher and a supportive institution. We are moving into an era where the individual learning design that characterized elitist education in the past can be combined with the equality of opportunity sought by the present system of group instruction.

The challenge of work, learning and leisure requires as a response the enlargement of our concept of public education. We have to extend it in time to include young children, post-secondary students, young adults, workers, and seniors. We must also extend it in scope to include the community activities sponsored by local government, the learning activities of voluntary organizations, training programs in business and industry, the activities of cultural institutions such as libraries, theatres, and museums, and the work of the media, especially educational television networks.

This is what continuing education really means. It does not mean incorporating all learning into the current concept of schooling; on the contrary, it promotes the reverse, the affirmation of many learning environments, formal and non-formal, that can promote learning, parallel to the many structures that can promote health, welfare, fitness, and the arts. Educational development is one aspect of social and cultural development and it must be integrated into these broader plans and policies.

Public education must place more emphasis on the challenge of finding and establishing meaning in a complex and rapidly changing society. This task has both an intellectual and a moral dimension. It involves exposing learners of all ages to the different meaning systems which have been developed to explain the world and our place within it: religious beliefs, cultural traditions, philosophical systems, scientific structures and artistic insights. Through these we can find a way of reading the world and creating a place for ourselves. The search for meaning is also a moral adventure, one that requires a merging of our understanding of values and our commitment to these values, the praxis of thought and action.

Finally, the challenge of pluralism must be met by new forms of institutional balance, between common goals and diverse needs, unifying structures and individual initiatives. Intercultural education must go beyond the stage of being a strategy to ease the transition of minorities into the majority culture; it must be willing to risk cultural exchange and the possibility that the majority culture may learn something worthwhile from other cultures. This learning must not only be on the level of style and traditions but also at the deeper level of perceptions and embedded values. Insofar as learning institutions receive greater diversity of learners (in ethnicity, age, beliefs, expectations, interests) they will be provoked to respond in flexible and creative ways.

These challenges to public education are not easily appreciated and not easily engaged. Yet if public education does not rise to these challenges, it will decline in importance as a social institution and lose its moral authority to guide learning in our society.

Preparing for the Future

This brings us to the central question of this paper: To what extent is public education in Canada today preparing for the future? Is it studying the major social trends? Is it exploring various ways of responding to them? Are these issues finding their way onto the agenda of policy makers in Canadian education? Are the structures and services changing to meet the new challenges?

A person concerned with the future would look at Canadian education of the 1980s with a certain mixture of deep despair and guarded hope. On the one hand, there are many factors that discourage Canadian educators from engaging in a study of the present and in planning for the future. First, there is the fragmentation of authority and responsibility among certain departments of the federal government, certain national organizations provincial governments, provincial organizations, and local structures. Considering that the locus of power in Canadian education is at the provincial level, it is not surprising that most of the critical and planning functions in Canadian education take place within provinces, often with little knowledge of (or interest in) what is happening elsewhere. Thus the inclination to engage in systematic evaluation and planning is contingent upon provincial priorities and sensitivities; the priorities are usually specific and immediate, the sensitivities are usually broad and deep. National organizations are usually influenced by regional agendas and restrict themselves to safe issues of common concern and coordination of existing policies.

There is a second type of fragmentation in Canadian education, one that separates public elementary and secondary education from other areas: private education, post-secondary education, and adult education. Rarely are there occasions, structures or issues which stimulate these sectors of education to come together to exchange ideas and study common problems. This fragmentation is further exacerbated by the proliferation of specialized provincial and national organizations which tend to keep administrators, trustees, teachers, civil servants, professors, parents, students, and adult educators talking and thinking within their own groups but which rarely promote dialogue across groups. Finally, there are the distances between regions and across language groups, divisions that too often prevent especially those in English Canada from learning from and building upon what is being done in Quebec.

Third, public education in English Canada has a strong conservative and pragmatic bias, making it sceptical of 'blue sky speculation about the future' and anxious to avoid contentious policy debates. Public school administrators and policy makers prefer to seek technical solutions and adjustments rather than enter into substantial re-thinking, and most educators are inclined to be fatalistic about the inertia of public institutions. French Quebec is more attracted to conceptual frameworks, plans, broad policies, and public debate on educational issues, but pays less attention to strategies of implementation, and its preoccupation with the cultural and linguistic functions of schooling have often distracted it from other issues.

Finally, the policy agenda of public education in Canada has been full of other more manageable items: territorial jurisdiction, second language teaching, computers in schools, the structure and financing of school boards, declining enrolments, budget constraints, the impact of the Charter of Rights, and public criticism of poor quality. There has not been too much inclination, or energy, to engage 'big' issues.

Interest in the future of Canadian education has been modest in recent years. A number of local conferences have been organized by educational associations with titles which refer to a future direction or focus, but a future perspective is usually limited to a keynote address. Compared to other countries and to the work of international organizations such as UNESCO and OECD, and to Canadian writing on other aspects of future planning, there is very little writing in Canada on the future of education. Virtually no attention is paid to the future of education by organizations outside of education, and systematic analysis or planning plays a small part in the work of most educational organizations. There are few forums in which educators and those outside the profession come together to discuss future directions and choices. Few policy statements of provincial governments include statements about the future, though some government departments have looked at or commissioned studies which bear upon the future development of education. Rarely are links being made between future studies and practical educational policy. There appear to be very few innovative efforts or pilot projects which are trying out radical new ideas about schools, the use of communications technology, or integrated approaches to learning. And there is very little action that suggests public education in Canada is preparing for the changes that seem to be coming.

There are, nevertheless, some promising initiatives. A number of people in curriculum development are trying to come up with new ways of determining content, new criteria by which priorities in content may be determined, and new strategies for reviewing curriculum. Alberta's 1984 Review of Secondary Education Programs included a project on the future of Alberta; Alberta Education is attempting to develop a list of core concepts, attitudes and skills that should provide a unifying theme for all curricula. Saskatchewan's Curriculum and Instruction Review included a report *Toward the Year 2000* which summarized different views on future trends. One of the most thorough and thoughtful studies on the future of education in Canada has been the work of the Strategic Planning Task group of the Ontario Ministries of Education and of Colleges and Universities which published a report *Towards the Year 2000* in 1984 dealing with the context and the educational options for Ontario.

Other curriculum innovations have included the growing interest across Canada in the development of thinking skills, projects to improve teaching and school effectiveness, programs to identify innovative practices in schools (as in British Columbia) and study groups in many provinces examining the components of core programs (such as the work of the Superior Council of Education in Quebec). Some of the interesting work in core programs and generic skills for adults (in the Report of the Jean Commission in Quebec and in various Federal reports, for instance) may begin to influence thinking in public education as well.

The technologies of communication are having an effect on public elementary and secondary education through extensive programs in almost every province to support the introduction of microcomputers in schools, find or develop appropriate courseware, design courses on the use of computers, computer literacy and computer languages, and apply computers to such areas as vocational training. A second influence of new technologies on teaching methods is beginning to develop through services of educational technology at the school and school board levels, using computers in classrooms or laboratories to teach certain skills, provide practice exercises, enliven some topics, and enrich learning for more able students. Programs of distance education and those which use technology to expand access to learning are more widely used in the North (for example, by the Katavik School Board in Quebec for Inuit communities) and by certain specialized post-secondary institutions (community colleges and adult education institutes). Yet the powerful educational television programs such as Knowledge Network in B.C., TV Ontario, Radio-Québec) have been developed largely outside of the public education system. Despite provocative studies such as those sponsored jointly by the Canadian Commission for UNESCO and TV Ontario, the impact of the new technologies on public education is not yet appreciated by most educational leaders.

There has been considerable thinking about the changing relationships among learning, work and leisure and between formal and non-formal educational structures, but this thinking has taken place mainly by those in the area of adult education. The works of the Canadian Commission for UNESCO, the Canadian Association for Adult Education, and the Jean Commission in Quebec have underlined the importance of establishing broader frameworks of continuing education for considering the total learning needs of individual Canadians and those of Canadian society as a whole. They stress the importance of life-long education in a period of rapid change, the need to think in broader terms about questions of financing, programs and services, and the complementarity of formal institutions in the education system and non-formal learning environments in the private, public and voluntary sectors. Despite some overlap between 'regular' and 'adult education' in School Boards, community colleges and universities, and despite some integration of Government departments responsible for adult and youth sectors, there remains little linkage between learning for the young and learning for the adult. The teaching profession is divided between those who work in public elementary and secondary schools, those in colleges, those in universities, and those in adult education. Each sector is suspicious of the others; many adult educators seek to distance themselves from what they see to be the rigidity of the compulsory school system; many in public and post-secondary education see adult education as an appendage to the school system, or as a soft and amorphous area long on rhetoric and short on rigour.

Furthermore, while there are many innovative programs seeking to establish closer links between schools and the world of work, especially in technical and business programs, and between the school and its community, most public schools remain apart from the larger society. Few elementary schools cooperate with senior citizens' homes to bring together young children and older persons with mutual interests in story telling, art, drama, and the wonders of the world; few secondary schools invite adults to join with adolescents in regular programs that may have common appeal; few communities see their local school as a centre of resources and services for learning in the whole community, linked on a permanent basis with the community library, museum, shopping mall, community centre, church groups and cultural organizations. Expensive school facilities and talented teachers are not often available to the public.

Many schools are trying to fulfill their responsibility to help young people look for meaning in their lives. This is the inspiration for many parents to send their children to separate schools or to private schools with a religious orientation, and for other parents to expect of public schools a respect for and serious interest in their cultural heritage. French-speaking Canadians want their schools not only to teach their children their language but also to instill in them the meaning of their cultural heritage and its values; this is no less true for other ethnic and cultural groups, native peoples, new Canadians, and members of cultural communities, not excluding the English, that may be here for generations.

It is a difficult task for public schools to serve a variety of religious and cultural meaning systems, and to respect the sensitivities of people when dealing with issues of value and philosophy of life. Many courses in social studies, literature, the arts, and, of course, moral and religious instruction engage the larger questions of meaning. Many schools, in their extracurricular activities, engage specific issues of racism, sexism, death, ecology, war, materialism, individualism, political and business ethics, and personal growth; many other schools avoid any issue that carries the hint of controversy or runs the danger of objection from even the most narrow and doctrinaire interest group, choosing instead to be the bland leading the bland.

Public education has made strenuous efforts to respond to the growing demands of cultural, religious and ethnic pluralism. These efforts have included extension of services for French-speaking minorities outside of Quebec, the development of French immersion programs in all provinces, heritage programs in various cultures and languages, activities furthering intercultural education and respect, better counselling and services for girls, greater sensitivity to sexist and racist stereotypes in textbooks and teaching materials, and more serious interest in the education of native peoples.

Public schools in many places are also reflections of a dominant middle-class, white, English or French culture in a public system that remains in many ways paternalistic in spirit. Not many schools have allowed their culture and style to be modified in a substantial way by incorporating even some of the values of the Native, Japanese, West Indian, Vietnamese, or Chilean Canadians. Educational pluralism remains more comfortable on the level of teaching method and superficial folkways than on the deeper levels of assumptions and values that may challenge some of our beliefs that we hold as natural and normal.

Conclusion

From the double perspective of the future of Canada and the relationship between public education and its social context, I would suggest that public education in Canada is only beginning to address some of the central issues that are shaping the future of our country and that are in the process of challenging our assumptions, structures, institutions and policies for learning. Insofar as I am inclined to be realistic in my assessment of public education in Canada in the late 1980s, I am inclined to believe that (a) education is so deeply embedded in the assumptions and structures of the industrial past that it will not adjust fast enough or thoroughly enough to the changing social environment, (b) the shape of learning in the future will be more profoundly influenced by developments outside of public education (in the media, high-technology industries, voluntary sectors, alternative institutions) than by the initiatives within public education, and (c) the importance of public elementary and secondary education in Canada will decline as other institutions, other clientele, and other systems of resources and services assume a larger part in shaping the learning society of tomorrow.

Insofar as I support the values of public education, prefer the transformation of existing structures to radical breaks with the past, and am impressed by the way in which institutions can change, even rapidly and thoroughly, I am inclined to believe that, given leadership, stimulation and support, public education cannot only adapt to the challenges of the social trends but even provide leadership for the relatively smooth transition to a post-industrial Canada that is not only an information society but also a learning society as well — perhaps even a wise society...

Concluding Statement

David L. Johnston

One challenge emerges clearly from this conference on the quality of education. Can we, as a society, achieve both equality of opportunity and excellence? Is it possible to view these two concepts as complementary and not competitive? And, if we accept this challenge, what are the implications for education, for our universities and for ourselves as university administrators?

The concepts of equality of opportunity and the pursuit of excellence have long been part of the Canadian ethos. Perhaps no other society has given greater attention to the full and free opportunity for the individual to develop. In addition succeeding waves of immigrants have instilled in us great expectations, the need to aspire to advancement and the will to achieve. If these traditions are to continue to nourish and enrich our society, quality in our educational systems will be the single most important catalyst. If we are to have equality of opportunity and excellence too, it could hardly be more fitting than that our universities recognize their fundamental responsibilities in this challenge — through the assumption of a leadership role in the pursuit of quality education.

In relating this challenge to the lessons for our universities, and for University Presidents in particular, two specific observations can be made. The first is that we must give more careful attention to our Faculties of Education. In doing so, we should remember that our universities are heirs to a tradition that dates to the middle Ages when theology, as one of the medieval university's three core faculties, played much the same kind of role as that performed by the modern Faculty of Education. It is perhaps surprising, therefore, that education is a relative newcomer to the Canadian academy and, as such, has been neglected and isolated from the academic mainstream. Canadian universities have had plenty of experience in integrating other professional faculties into the arts and science core — law, medicine, engineering and management come to mind. The time has come to do the same with education and the benefits are not likely to be confined to the education faculty. If past experience is an example, we can expect this new relationship to result in a revitalization of the core faculties, providing us with new perspectives and new avenues for scholarship and research.

What is the most constructive and positive way to give Faculties of Education a central place within our institutions? I hope each of us will answer this for ourselves in collaboration with our colleagues in the Faculties of Education and in a manner most appropriate to our own institution. One approach that I believe holds great promise would have professors in the various arts and science disciplines linked to their counterparts (both professors and students) in the Faculty of Education. Each working team could have as its mandate the evaluation and improvement of education, at all levels, within their respective disciplines. By working together with a common sense of purpose, rather than as separate and disinterested parties, members of our arts and science and education faculties could contribute to an important new coherence in educational planning and evaluation.

The second observation relates to an understanding of how we learn. This understanding is fundamental to institutional responsibility for the advancement of learning in our society. It reaches from the level of the individual through to our education systems. In Canada, we should relish the rich diversity that is our legacy. Our linguistic heritage goes beyond our two official languages to include the languages of our Native Peoples and successive groups of new Canadians. We provide for both secular and religious schools and institutions. Our experience is enriched by the diversity of provincial systems and by a Canada-wide university network that is enormously diverse in the size, orientation and research stengths of its institutions.

Moreover as the world's most active trading nation and one that has made exceptional efforts to preserve ethnic heritage, Canada is particularly well placed to study more attentively and completely the educational lessons of other jurisdictions that have wrestled with quality in their educational systems. The influence on our systems of the British, the French and the American experiences is reasonably well established. But there are many other experiences to be studied and from which we might profitably adapt and implant lessons.

It is timely for us to look at what others are doing and apply their teaching where applicable. Just as I was finishing this note, *The President's Report for 1985–86* from Harvard University arrived on my desk. President Bok begins his report in this way:

> In 1983, the National Commission on Excellence in Education issued a scathing indictment of the nation's public schools that touched off a spirited debate on schooling in America. The

Commission spoke harshly of a 'rising tide of mediocrity' in our public schools and accused the society of engaging in a process of 'unilateral educational disarmament'. Since then, more reports have been issued, books have been written, and innumerable articles on educational reform have appeared in our daily newspapers. Spurred by the interest that these criticisms have aroused, many states have taken steps to improve the quality of their public schools by raising teachers' salaries, tightening academic standards, and improving curricular requirements.

Yet there is a curious side to this debate. The institutions most responsible for inquiring into the nature of public education are the professional schools of education set in our leading research universities. One would have thought, therefore, that the attention lavished on the schools would raise the profile of these faculties and make them centres of activity and attention. Quite the contrary. The many reports and studies that have emerged make little mention of these professional schools. Members of their faculties have played only a small part in the commissions that have been so prominent in the public discussions. The surging interest in the schools has likewise failed to lift the stature of education faculties on campus; if anything the reverse has been true. Within the past few years, Duke University closed its department of education, Michigan cut back its faculty substantially, and Berkeley's education school was saved only by a last minute reprieve from the Chancellor.

Why are these faculties relegated to the margins of the university, fighting for their existence at a time when they should occupy center stage in the national effort to improve our public schools? What can they do — and what is Harvard's Faculty of Education doing — to play a role commensurate with the importance that America attaches to their central field of interest?[1]

The balance of his report touches directly upon the issues contained in this book and focuses the attention of his university on the important role of its Faculty of Education.

The AUCC conference of March 1987 itself signalled a new challenge for Canadian universities. From it will emerge an AUCC statement of principles for quality education in Canada. The process of preparing, debating and seeking approval and support for that statement will be enormously beneficial to the university Presidents who will address this important issue and, we hope, to the prospects for an improved system of quality education. Once completed, the statement will assist the Association and individual universities to pursue, with renewed vigour, the challenge of maintaining an educational system grounded on the two principles of excellence and equality of opportunity. The papers in this volume provide an important framework from which to take up that challenge.

Notes

[1]D. Bok, *The President's Report 1985–86.* (Boston: Harvard University, 1987), pp. 1–2.

Select Bibliography

ALBERTA EDUCATION. *Review of Secondary Programs*. III vols. Edmonton: Alberta Education, 1984.

ANDERSON, A.B. and FRIDERES, J.S. *Ethnicity in Canada: Theoretical Perspectives*. Toronto: Butterworths, 1981.

ANDERSON, B. D. *et al. The Cost of Controlling the Costs of Education in Canada*. Toronto: Ontario Institute for Studies in Education Press, 1983.

ANDREWS, J. H. M and ROGERS, W. T. (eds.) *Canadian Research in Education: A State of the Art Review*. Ottawa: Supply and Services Canada, 1982.

ANISEF, P. *et al. Accessibility to Post-Secondary Education in Canada: A Review of the Literature*. Ottawa: Education Support Branch, Department of the Secretary of State, 1986.

APPLE, M. 'Curriculum in the Year 2000: Tensions and Possibilities.' *Phi Delta Kappan*, vol. 64 no. 5 (1983), pp. 321–326.

ARMOUR, L. and TROTT, E. *The Faces of Reason: An Essay on Philosophy and Culture in English Canada, 1850–1950*. Waterloo: Wilfrid Laurier University Press, 1981.

ASTIN, A.W. *Achieving Educational Excellence*. San Francisco: Jossey-Bass, 1985.

ASTIN, A.W. *et al. The American Freshman: National Norms and Fall 1984*. Los Angeles. Higher Education Research Institute, Graduate School of Education, University of California, 1984.

ATKIN, J.M. 'American Graduate Schools of Education: A View from Abroad.' *Oxford Review of Education*, vol. 9 no. 1 (1983), pp. 63–69.

BENNIS, W. and NAMUS, B. *Leaders: The Strategies for Taking Charge*. New York: Harper and Row, 1985.

BERCUSON, D.J., BOTHWELL, R. and GRANATSTEIN, J.L. *The Great Brain Robbery: Canada's Universities on the Road to Ruin*. Toronto: McClelland and Stewart, 1984.

BIBBY, R. and POSTERSKI, D. *The Emerging Generation*. Toronto: Irwin, 1985.

BLANEY, J.P. 'Extension and the University: A Clash of Cultures.' *Canadian Journal of University Continuing Education*, vol. XII no. 1 (February, 1986).

BLANEY, J.P. 'Leaders in University Continuing Education: Challenges, Opportunities and Tasks,' a paper in manuscript presented to The Canadian Association for Continuing Education, 1986.

BRETON, R. *Cultural Boundaries and the Cohesion of Canada*. Montreal: Institute for Research on Public Policy, 1980.

CANADA, BADGLEY COMMISSION. *Sexual Offences Against Children: Report of the Commission on Sexual Offences Against Children and Youths*. Ottawa: Canadian Government Publishing Centre, 1984.

CANADA, MACDONALD COMMISSION. *Report of the Royal Commission on the Economic*

Union and Development Prospects for Canada. 3 vols. Ottawa: Supply and Services Canada, 1985.

CANADA, SECRETARY of STATE. *Federal and Provincial Support to Post-Secondary Education in Canada: A Report to Parliament, 1985–86.* Ottawa: Supply and Services Canada, 1987.

CANADA TOMORROW CONFERENCE. *Commissioned Papers.* Ottawa: Supply and Services Canada, 1984.

CANADA TOMORROW CONFERENCE. *Proceedings.* Ottawa: Supply and Services Canada, 1984.

CANADIAN BUREAU OF INTERNATIONAL EDUCATION. *Closing the Doors? A Statistical Report on International Students in Canada 1983–85.* Ottawa: CBIE, 1986.

CANADIAN COMMISSION FOR UNESCO. *Adult Literacy in Canada: A Challenge.* Occasional Paper 42. Ottawa: The Commission, 1983.

CANADIAN COMMISSION FOR UNESCO. *Learning in Society.* Occasional Paper 41. Ottawa: The Commission, 1983.

CANADIAN EDUCATION ASSOCIATION. *Marketing The School System: Building Public Confidence in Schools.* Toronto: CEA, 1986.

CANADIAN EDUCATION ASSOCIATION. *Speaking Out; The 1984 CEA Poll of Canadian Opinion On Education.* Toronto: CEA, 1984.

CARNEGIE FORUM ON EDUCATION AND THE ECONOMY. *A Nation Prepared: Teachers for the 21st Century, the Report of the Task Force on Teaching as a Profession.* New York: Carnegie Forum, 1986.

CETRON, M. *Schools of the Future.* New York: McGraw-Hill, 1985.

CLIFFORD, D.K. JR. AND CAVANAGH, R.E. *The Winning Performance.* Toronto: Bantam Books, 1985.

ᴖCLOUTIER, R. *et al.* (eds.) *Analyse sociale de l'éducation.* Montreal : Boreal Express, 1983.

COHEN, D. and SHANNON, K. *The NEXT Canadian Economy.* Montreal: Eden Press, 1984.

CONNELL, G.E. 'Vital Links between Schools and Universities.' *The Graduate,* vol. XIII no. 4 (1986), pp. 24–25.

CONTINUING EDUCATION REVIEW PROJECT. *Project Report: For Adults Only.* Toronto: Ministry of Colleges and Universities, 1986.

COOMBS, P.H. *The World Crisis in Education: The View from the Eighties.* London: Oxford University Press, 1985.

CORDELL, A. *The Uneasy Eighties: The Transition to an Information Society.* Background Study No. 53, Ottawa: Science Council of Canada, 1985.

COUNCIL OF MINISTERS OF EDUCATION, CANADA. *A New Deal in Minority Language Education. The State of Minority Language Education in the Provinces and Territories of Canada.* Toronto: CMEC, 1983.

COUNCIL OF MINISTERS OF EDUCATION, CANADA. *Changing Economic Circumstances: The Challenge for Postsecondary Education and Manpower Training.* Toronto: CMEC, 1985.

COUNCIL OF MINISTERS OF EDUCATION, CANADA. *Principles for Interaction: Federal-Provincial Relations and Postsecondary Education in Canada.* Toronto: CMEC, 1985.

COUNCIL OF MINISTERS OF EDUCATION, CANADA. *Education in Canada 1984–1986, Report to the 40th Session, International Conference on Education, Geneva.* Toronto: CMEC, 1986.

COUNCIL OF MINISTERS OF EDUCATION, CANADA. *Post-secondary Education Issues in the 1980s.* Toronto: CMEC, 1983.

COUNCIL OF ONTARIO UNIVERSITIES. *Report of the Special Committee on Teacher Education.* Toronto: COU, 1984.

CROSS, K.P. 'New Students in New Bottles,' in William A.W. Neilsen and Chad Gaffield

(Eds) *Universities in Crisis: A Medieval Institution in the Twenty-first Century.*
Montreal: Institute for Research on Public Policy, 1986.

CROSS, K.P. 'The Changing Role of Higher Education in the Learning Society.'
Continuum, vol. 49 no. 2 (Spring 1985).

CYERT, R.M. 'Academic Leadership.' *Continuum*, vol. 49 no. 2 (Spring 1985).

DARLING–HAMMOND, L. *Beyond the Commission Reports: The Coming Crisis in
Teaching.* Santa Monica: Rand Corporation, 1984.

DECORE, A.M. and PANNU, R.S. 'Educational Financing in Canada 1970–71 to 1984–85:
Who Calls the Tune, Who Pays the Piper?' *The Canadian Journal of Higher
Education*, vol. XVI no. 2 (1986), pp. 27–49.

DENNISON, J.D. and GALLAGHER, P. *Canada's Community Colleges: A Critical Analysis.*
Vancouver: University of British Columbia Press, 1986.

DEVEREAUX, M.S. *One in Every Five: A Survey of Adult Education in Canada.* Ottawa:
Statistics Canada and the Department of the Secretary of State, 1985.

DRESSEL, D.L. *Administrative Leadership.* San Francisco: Jossey Bass, 1981.

DRUCKER, P. *Innovation and Entrepreneurship.* New York: Harper and Row, 1985.

ELLUL, J. *The Technological Society.* New York: Vintage Books, 1964.

EURICH, N.P. *Corporate Classrooms: The Learning Business.* Princeton, N.J.: The
Carnegie Foundation for the Advancement of Teaching, 1985.

FEIGENBAUM, E. and McCORDUCK, P. *The Fifth Generation: Artificial Intelligence and
Japan's Computer Challenge to the World.* Reading, Mass.: Addison-Wesley, 1983.

FLEMING, T. 'Restraints, Reform and Reallocation.' *Education Canada*, vol. 25 no. 1
(1985), pp. 4–11.

FLORMAN, S.C. *Blaming Technology: The Irrational Search for Scapegoats.* New York:
St. Martin's Press, 1981.

FOOT, D.K. 'Youth Employment in Canada: A Misplaced Priority?' *Canadian Public
Policy*, vol. XII no. 3 (1986), pp. 499–506.

FOREST, M. *Education/Integration.* Toronto: National Institute on Mental Retardation,
1984.

FORTUNE, R. 'School–College Collaboration Programs in English,' in Joseph Gibaldi ed.
Options for Teaching. Chicago: Modern Language Association of America, 1986.

FOSTER, W.F. 'Educational Malpractice: A Tort for the Untaught?' *University of British
Columbia Law Review*, vol. 19 (1985), pp. 161–244.

FRIESEN, J.W. *When Cultures Clash: Case Studies in Multiculturalism.* Calgary:
Detselig, 1985.

FULLAN, M. *The Meaning of Educational Change.* Toronto: Ontario Institute for
Studies in Education Press, 1982.

FULLAN, M. AND CONNELLY, F.M. *Teacher Education in Ontario: Current Practice and
Options for the Future.* Toronto: Ministry of Education/Ministry of Colleges and
Universities, 1987.

GAFFIELD, C. 'Coherence and Chaos in Educational Historiography.' *Interchange*, vol.
17. no. 2 (Summer, 1986), pp. 112–121.

GAFFIELD, C. 'History of Education,' in *The Canadian Encyclopedia.* vol. 1 Edmonton:
Hurtig, 1985, pp. 546–47.

GARDNER, J.W. 'The Nature of Leadership,' in *Leadership Papers/1.* Washington, D.C.:
Independent Sector, 1986.

GARDNER, J.W. 'The Tasks of Leadership,' in *Leadership Papers/2.* Washington, D.C.:
Indt: Educating Canadians for Towmorrow's World. Report 36, Hull, Quebec:
Canadian Government Publishing Centre, 1984.

GHOSH, R. AND RAY, D. (eds.) *Social Change and Education in Canada.* Toronto:
Harcourt Brace Jovanovich, 1987.

GILDER, G. *The Spirit of Enterprise.* New York: Simon and Schuster, 1984.

GODET, M. *Crises Are Opportunities.* Montreal: GAMMA, 1985.

GODFREY, D. AND PARKHILL, D. (eds.) *Gutenberg Two: The New Electronics and Social*

Change. Toronto: Press Porcépic, 1980.

GOODLAD, J. *A Place Called School.* Toronto: McGraw-Hill, 1984.

GOULET, J. *Les répercussions culturelles de l'informatisation au Québec.* Québec: Conseil de la langue française, 1982.

GRAPKO, M. *The Role of Faculties of Education in the Implementation and Evaluation of Educational Change: Feasibility Study, Phase I.* Toronto: Ontario Ministry of Education, 1986.

GREEN, T. *The Formation of Conscience in an Age of Technology.* Syracuse: Syracuse University Press, 1984.

GRIMMETT, P.P. *Resarch in Teacher Education: Current Problems and Future Prospects in Canada.* Vancouver: Centre for the Study of Curriculum and Instruction, University of British Columbia, 1984.

GROS LOUIS, K.R.R. 'Making a Beginning: Adults Learners and the 21st Century University.' *Continuum,* vol. 49 no. 2 (Spring 1985).

GUPPY, N. *et al.* 'Changing Patterns of Educational Inequality in Canada.' *Canadian Journal of Sociology,* vol. 9 no. 3 (1984), pp. 319–321.

HAMBURGER, P. 'Profiles (Vartan Gregorian — Part II).' *New Yorker,* (April 21, 1986).

HARRIGAN, P.J. 'A Comparative Perspective on Recent Trends in the History of Education in Canada.' *History of Education Quarterly,* vol. 26 no. 1 (Spring, 1986). pp. 71–86.

HENCHEY, N. AND BURGESS, D.A. *Between Past and Future: Quebec Education in Transition.* Calgary: Detselig, 1987.

HENCHEY, N. *Education for the 21st Century: Canadian Imperatives.* Ottawa: Canadian Teachers' Federation, 1983.

HENCHEY, N. 'La revolution des communications.' *Prospectives,* vol. 19 (1983), pp. 25–31.

HENCHEY, N. 'Means and Ends: The Reduction of Curriculum to Technique.' *McGill Journal of Education,* vol. 18 (1983), pp. 253–270.

HENCHEY, N. 'Rethinking Learning.' *Policy Options,* vol. 7 no. 2 (1986), pp. 20–22.

HERROLD, E. *Sexual Behaviour of Canadian Young People.* Markham, Ontario: Fitzhenry and Whiteside, 1984.

HERSOM, N., BIRCH, D. and GASKELL, J. *Research in Teacher Education: State of the Art.* Report to the Social Sciences and Humanities Research Council of Canada. Vancouver: University of British Columbia. 1982.

HICKMAN, C.R. AND SILVA, M.A. *Creating Excellence.* New York: NAL books, 1984.

HILLER, H.H. *Canadian Society: A Macro Analysis.* Scarborough, Ontario: Prentice-Hall, 1986.

HOLDAWAY, E.A. 'Educational Research in Canada,' in J. Nisbet, J. Megarry, and S. Nishbet, (eds.) *World Yearbook of Education 1985: Research, Policy and Practice.* London: Kogan Page, 1985, pp. 79–94.

HOLMES GROUP. *Tomorrow's Teachers.* East Lansing: The Holmes Group, Inc., 1986.

HOUGH, J.R. (ed.) *Educational Policy: An International Survey.* London: groom Helm, 1984.

HOWEY, K.R. AND GARDNER W.E., *The Education of Teachers.* New York: Longman, 1983.

HUSEN, T. AND KOGAN, M. (eds.) *Educational Research and Policy: How Do They Relate?* Oxford: Pergamon Press, 1984.

IVANY, J.W. AND MANLEY-CASIMIR, M.E. (eds.) *Federal-Provincial Relations: Education Canada.* Toronto: Ontario Institute for Studies in Education Press, 1981.

JOHNSTON, J.S. JR. *et al. Educating Managers: Executive Effectiveness Through Liberal Learning.* San Francisco: Jossey Bass, 1986.

JOHNSTON, R. *Public Opinion and Public Policy in Canada.* Toronto: University of Toronto Press, 1986.

JONES, D.C., *et al.*, (eds.) *Approaches to Educational History*. Winnipeg: University of Manitoba, 1981.

JUDGE, H. *American Graduate Schools of Education: A View from Abroad*. New York: Ford Foundation, 1982.

KACH, N. *et al.* (eds.) *Essays on Canadian Education*. Calgary: Detselig, 1986.

KANTER, R.M. *The Change Masters*. New York: Simon and Schuster, 1983.

KILIAN, C. *School Wars: The Assault on B.C. Education*. Vancouver: New Star Books, 1985.

KILMAN, R.H. *Beyond the Quick Fix*. San Francisco: Jossey Bass, 1984.

KROKER, A. *Technology and the Canadian Mind: Innis, McLuhan Grant*. Montreal: New World Perspectives, 1984.

LaROCQUE, L. *Policy Implementation in a School District: A Matter of Chance?* Burnaby, B.C.: Simon Fraser University, 1983.

LaROCQUE, L. AND COLEMAN, P. 'The Elusive Link: School-Level Responses to School Board Policies.' *Alberta Journal of Educational Research*, vol. 31 no. 2 (1985), pp. 149–167.

Le Groupe Québécois de Prospective. *Le future du Québec au conditionnel*. Chicoutimi: Gaetan Morin, 1982.

LIVINGSTONE, D.W. *Class Ideologies and Educational Futures*. Sussex: Falmer Press, 1983.

LIVINGSTONE, D.W. (ed.) *Critical Pedagogy and Cultural Power*. South Hadley, Mass.: Bergin and Garvey, 1987.

LIVINGSTONE, D.W. *Social Crisis and Schooling*. Toronto: Garamond Press, 1985.

MACCOBY, M. *The Leader*. New York: Simon and Schuster, 1981.

MACDONALD, J.W. *Teacher Education in Ontario, Report to the International Advisory Panel, Chinese Provincial Universities Development Project*. Washington, D.C.: World Bank, 1986.

MACKAY, A.W. *Education Law In Canada*. Toronto: Emond-Montgomery, 1984.

MACKAY, A.W. 'The Canadian Charter of Rights and Freedoms: A Springboard to Students' Rights.' *Windsor Yearbook of Access to Justice*, vol. 4 (1984), pp. 174–228.

MACKAY, A.W. 'The Equality Provisions of the Charter and Education: A Structural Analysis.' *Canadian Journal of Education*, vol. 11 no. 3 (1986), pp. 293–312.

MACNEIL, T. 'Challenges and Opportunities In Canadian Adult Education.' *Learning*, vol. IV no. 3 (1986), pp. 8–11.

MAGNUSON, R. *A Brief History of Quebec Education*. Montreal: Harvest House, 1980.

MALLEA, J.R. AND YOUNG, J.C. *Cultural Diversity and Canadian Education*. Don Mills, Ontario: Oxford University Press, 1984.

MANLEY-CASIMIR, M. AND SUSSEL, T. (eds.) *Courts in the Classroom: Education and the Charter of Rights and Freedoms*. Calgary: Detselig, 1986.

MARCH, M.E. AND MIKLOS, E. 'Dynamics of Control Over Educational Decisions.' *Alberta Journal of Educational Research*, vol. 29 no. 1 (1983), pp. 1–14.

MARTIN, W.B.W. AND MACDONNELL, A.J. (eds.) *Canadian Education: A Sociological Analysis*. Scarborough, Ontario: Prentice-Hall, 1982.

MASUDA, Y. *The Information Society as Post-Industrial Society*. Washington, D.C.: World Future Society, 1980.

McCORKLE, C.O. JR AND ARCHIBALD, S.D. *Management and Leadership in Higher Education*. San Francisco: Jossey Bass, 1982.

McKILLOP, A.B. *A Disciplined Intelligence*. Montreal: McGill-Queen's University Press, 1979.

McLEAN, L. *et al.* (eds.) *Research on Teaching in Canada*. Toronto: Ontario Institute for Studies in Education Press, 1982.

MINTZBERG, H. *The Structuring of Organizations*. Englewood Cliffs, N.J.: Prentice Hall, 1979.

MUNGER, P.D. 'Future Academic Leadership: Challenges to Continuing Higher Education.' *Continuum*, vol. 49 no. 2 (Spring 1985).

MYERS, D. (ed.) *The Failure of Educational Reform in Canada.* Toronto: McClelland and Stewart, 1973.

NAISBITT, J. *Megatrends: Ten New Directions Transforming Our Lives.* New York: Warner, 1982.

NAISBITT, J. AND ABURDENE, P. *Re-inventing the Organization.* New York: Warner, 1985.

NATIONAL COMMISSION FOR EXCELLENCE IN TEACHER EDUCATION. *A Call for Change in Teacher Education.* Washington, D.C.: American Association of Colleges of Teacher Education, 1985.

NATIONAL COMMISSION ON EXCELLENCE IN EDUCATION. *A Nation At Risk: The Imperative For Educational Reform.* Washington, D.C.: U.S. Government Printing Office, 1983.

NATIONAL COMMISSION ON EXCELLENCE IN EDUCATION. *The Nation Responds: Recent Efforts to Improve Education.* Washington, D.C.: U.S. Department of Education, 1984.

NATIONAL COUNCIL ON WELFARE. *Poor Kids.* Ottawa: NCW, 1985.

NATIONAL COUNCIL ON WELFARE. *Poverty Profile.* Ottawa: NCW, 1985.

NEATBY, H. *So Little for the Mind.* Toronto: Clarke Irwin, 1953.

NELSEN, R. 'Books, Boredom and Behind Bars: An Explanation of Apathy and Hostility in Our Schools.' *Canadian Journal of Education*, vol. 10 no. 2 (1985), pp. 136–160.

ONTARIO, COMMISSION ON THE FUTURE DEVELOPMENT OF THE UNIVERSITIES OF ONTARIO. *Options and Futures.* Toronto: Ministry of Education/Ministry of Colleges and Universities, 1984.

ONTARIO. *Report of Secondary Education Review Project.* Toronto: Ministry of Education/Ministry of Colleges and Universities, 1981.

ONTARIO. 'TOWARDS THE YEAR 2000: FUTURE CONDITIONS AND STRATEGIC OPTIONS FOR THE SUPPORT OF LEARNING IN ONTARIO.' *Review and Evaluation Bulletin*, vol. 5 no. 1 (1984).

ORGANIZATION FOR ECONOMIC CO-OPERATION AND DEVELOPMENT. *Education in Modern Society.* Paris: OECD, 1985.

ORGANIZATION FOR ECONOMIC CO-OPERATION AND DEVELOPMENT. *New Information Technologies: A Challenge for Education.* Paris: OECD, 1986.

ORGANIZATION FOR ECONOMIC CO-OPERATION AND DEVELOPMENT. *Reviews of National Policies for Education: Canada.* Paris: OECD, 1976.

ORPWOOD, G.W.F. and SOUGE, J.-P. *Science Education in Canadian Schools.* Ottawa: Science Council of Canada, 1984.

O'TOOLE, J. *Vanguard Management: Redesigning the Corporate Future.* Garden City, N.Y.: Doubleday, 1985.

OWRAM, D. *The Government Generation: Canadian Intellectuals and the State, 1900–1945.* Toronto: University of Toronto Press, 1986.

PAPERT, S. *Mindstorms: Children, Computers and Powerful Ideas.* New York: Basic Books, 1980.

PERELMAN, L.J. 'Learning our Lesson: Why School Is Out.' *The Futurist*, vol. 20 no. 2 (1986), pp. 13–16.

PETER, T.J. and WATERMAN, R.H. JR. *In Search of Excellence.* New York: Harper and Row, 1982.

PETERS, T. and AUSTIN, N. *A Passion for Excellence.* New York: Random House, 1985.

PHILLIPS, C.E. *The Development of Education in Canada.* Toronto: W.J. Gage, 1957.

PORTER, J. et al. *Stations and Callings: Making It Through the School System.* Toronto: Methuen, 1982.

PORTER, M.E. *Competitive Advantage.* New York: The Free Press, 1985.

QUÉBEC. *La formation fondamentale et la qualité de l'éducation.* Québec: Counseil Supérieur de l'Éducation, 1984.

QUÉBEC. *Learning: A Voluntary and Responsible Action, Summary Report of the Commission d'étude sur la formation des adultes.* M. Jean, Chairperson. Québec: CEFA, 1982.

RATSOY, E.W., BABCOCK, G.R. and CALDWELL, J.C. *Evaluation of the Education Practicum Program 1977–1978.* Edmonton: University of Alberta, 1978.

RAVITCH, D. *The Schools We Deserve.* New York: Basic Books, 1985.

RAY, D. AND D'OYLEY, V. (eds.) *Human Rights in Canadian Education.* Dubuque, Iowa: Kandell/Hunt, 1984.

ROGERS, W.T. AND McLEAN, L.D. 'Promoting Federal Support for Education Research.' *Educational Researcher,* vol. 16 no. 2 (1987). pp. 10–15.

RUSH, C. AND EVERS, F.T. *Making The Match: Canada's University Graduates and Corporate Employers.* Montreal: Corporate-Higher Education Forum, 1986.

SASKATCHEWAN. *Curriculum and Instruction Review: Directions, The Final Report and Toward the Year 2000.* Regina: Saskatchewan Education, 1984.

SCHEIN, E.H. *Organizational Culture and Leadership.* San Francisco: Jossey Bass, 1985.

SCIENCE COUNCIL OF CANADA. *Planning Now for an Information Society: Tomorrow Is Too Late.* Ottawa: Supply and Services Canada, 1982.

SCIENCE COUNCIL OF CANADA. *Science for Every Student: Educating Canadians for Tomorrow's World.* Report 36, Hull, Quebec: Canadian Government Publishing Centre, 1984.

SECRETAN, L. H.K. *Managerial Moxie.* Toronto: Holt, Rinehart and Winston, 1986.

SEGAL, B. 'Corporate–Higher Education Partnerships,' an address to the 1985 Annual Meeting of the Canadian Association for University Continuing Education, Ottawa, June, 1985.

SHANE, H.G. 'The Silicone Age and Education.' *Phi Delta Kappan,* vol. 63 (1982), pp. 303–308.

SHANE, H.G. with TABLER, M.B. *Educating for a New Millennium.* Bloomington, Ind.: Phi Delta Kappa, 1981.

SHANNON, D.W. 'Traditional Students and Adults: Are They Fundamentally Alike in All Unimportant Particulars?' *The Journal of Continuing Higher Education,* vol. 34 no. 2 (Spring 1986), pp. 8–12.

SHAPIRO, B.J. (Commissioner), *Report of the Commission on Private Schools in Ontario.* Toronto: Ministry of Education, 1985.

SHAPIRO, B.J. 'Scholarly Concerns of a Faculty of Education.' *The Journal of Educational Thought,* vol. 19 no. 1 (1985), pp. 40–48.

SHEEHAN, N.M., WILSON, J.D. and JONES, D.C. (eds.) *Schools in the West: Essays in Canadian Educational History.* Calgary : Detselig, 1986.

SHEFFIELD, E. et al. *Systems of Higher Education: Canada.* New York: International Council for Educational Development, 1982.

SHEFFIELD, E. *Research on Post-secondary Education in Canada.* Ottawa: Supply and Services Canada, 1982.

SKILL DEVELOPMENT LEAVE TASK FORCE. *Learning A Living in Canada.* 2 vols. Ottawa: Employment and Immigration Canada, 1983.

SOCIAL SCIENCES AND HUMANITIES RESEARCH COUNCIL OF CANADA. *Annual Report 1984–85.* Ottawa: Supply and Services Canada, 1985.

SPECIAL SENATE COMMITTEE ON YOUTH. *Youth: A Plan of Action.* Ottawa: Senate of Canada, 1986.

SPRAAKMAN, G., BECHER, T. and WILDE, K. (eds.) *Canadian Cultural Futures: Options for Living Together.* Montreal: Canadian Association for Future Studies, 1984.

STAPLETON, J.J., ALLARD, M. and MacIVER, D.A. *Education Research in Canada: Aims, Problems and Possibilities.* Ottawa: Supply and Services Canada, 1982.

STATISTICS CANADA. *Schooling in Canada.* Ottawa: Statistics Canada, 1984.

STEVENSON, H.A. and WILSON J.D. (eds.) *Precepts, Policy and Process: Perspectives on Contemporary Canadian Education.* London: Alexander, Blake Associates, 1977.

Select Bibliography

STEVENSON, H.A. 'Ten Years to Know-where,' in Douglas Myers (ed.) *The Failure of Educational Reform in Canada*. Toronto: McClelland and Stewart, 1973, pp. 50–59.

STEWIN, L. and McCANN, S. (eds.) *Contemporary Educational Issues: A Canadian Mosaic*. Toronto: Copp Clark Pitman, 1987.

SUTHERLAND, N. *Children in English–Canadian Society: Framing the Twentieth Century Consensus*. Toronto: University of Toronto Press, 1976.

SYMONS, T.H.B. 'Canadian Post-secondary Education: The Cultural Agenda,' in Alexander Gregor and Keith Wilson (eds.) *Post-secondary Education in Canada: The Cultural Agenda I*. Winnipeg: The University of Manitoba, 1986.

TOBIN, J. and SHARON, D. *New Technologies in Education in Canada: Issues and Concerns*. Paper 17 in a series on *New Technologies in Canadian Education*. Toronto: TV Ontario and the Canadian Commission for UNESCO, 1984.

TOBIN, J. *The High Technology Industry and Education in Canada*. Paper 16 in a series on *New Technologies in Canadian Education*. Toronto: TV Ontario and the Canadian Commission for UNESCO, 1984.

TOMKINS, G.S. *A Common Countenance: Stability and Change in the Canadian Curriculum*. Scarborough, Ontario: Prentice-Hall, 1986.

TURKLE, S. *The Second Self: Computers and the Human Spirit*. New York: Simon & Schuster, 1984.

TURRITTIN, A.H. *et al.* "Gender Differences in Educational Achievement: A Study of Social Inequality." *Canadian Journal of Sociology*, vol. 8 no. 4 (1983), pp. 395–419.

UNITED NATIONS EDUCATIONAL, SCIENTIFIC AND CULTURAL ORGANIZATION. *Reflections on the Future Development of Education*. paris: UNESCO, 1985.

UNITED NATIONS EDUCATIONAL, SCIENTIFIC AND CULTURAL ORGANZATION. *The Social Implications of the Scientific and Technological Revolution*. Paris: UNESCO, 1981.

UNITED STATES DEPARTMENT OF EDUCATION. *Japanese Education Today*. Washington, D.C.: U.S. Government Printing Office, 1984.

UNIVERSITY OF BRITISH COLUMBIA. *Background to and Rationale for the Revised Teacher Education Program*. Vancouver: Faculty of Education (Internal Document), 1986.

UNIVERSITY OF CALGARY. *The Shrinking Maze: Report of the University Program Review Committee*. Calgary: The University of Calgary, 1980.

UNRAH, W. *Evaluation of the Faculty of Education*. Calgary: University of Calgary, 1981.

VAILLANCOURT, F. and HENRIQUES, I. 'The Returns to University Schooling in Canada.' *Canadian Public Policy*, vol. XII no. 3 (1986), pp. 449–458.

VALASHAKIS, K. *The Information Society: The Issues and the Choices, Integrating Report, Phase I. GAMMA Information Society Project*. Montreal: GAMMA, 1979.

VANDERBURG, W.H. (ed.) *Perspectives on Our Age: Jacques Ellul Speaks on His Life and Works*. Toronto: Canadian Broadcasting Corporation, 1981.

VAN FOSSEN, R.W. *Report of the OS:IS Liaison Officer, September 1985 – August 1986*. Toronto: Council of Ontario Universities, 1986.

VICE, D. *Post-Secondary Education in Canada: A Capital Investment — An Address to the Senate Committee on Finance*. Mississaugua, Ontario: Northern/Telecom, 1986.

WAGNER, S. 'Illiteracy and Adult Literacy Teaching in Canada.' *Prospects*, vol. 15 no. 3 (1985).

WIDEEN, M. and HOLBORN, P. 'Research in Canadian Teacher Education.' *Canadian Journal of Education*, vol. 11 (1986), pp. 557–583.

WILKINSON, B.W. 'Elementary and Secondary Education Policy in Canada: A Survey.' *Canadian Public Policy*, vol. XII no. 4 (1986), pp. 535–72.

WILSON, J.D. (ed.) *An Imperfect Past: Education and Society in Canadian History*. Vancouver: University of British Columbia Curriculum Centre, 1984.

WILSON, J.D. (ed.) *Canadian Education in the 1980's.* Calgary: Detselig, 1981.

WILSON, J.D., STAMP, R.M. and AUDET, L.-P. (eds.) *Canadian Education: A History.* Scarborough: Prentice-Hall, 1970.

WINCHESTER, I., HOLMES, M. and OLIVER, H. (eds.) 'Illuminating Education: The Uses of Science, History and Philosophy in Educational Thought.' Anniversary issue of *Interchange,* vol. 17 no. 2 (1986).

WIPPER, A. (ed.) *The Sociology of Work.* Ottawa: Carleton University Press, 1984.

WISE, A.E. *Legislated Learning.* Berkeley: University of California Press, 1979.

WISENTHAL, M. *Education Research: Future Expectations and Past Performance.* Ottawa: Supply and Services Canada, 1982.

WOTHERSPOON, T. (ed.) *The Political Economy of Canadian Schooling.* Toronto: Methuen, 1987.

WUESTER, T.J. 'The Harmonization of School Legislation in Canada,' in R.C.C. Cuming. (ed.) *Perspectives on The Harmonization of Law in Canada.* Toronto: University of Toronto Press, 1985, pp. 117–158.

Index

1